"David and Lisa provide tested and trusted insights that will help any marriage better honor God and experience all the joy and fulfillment He intended when He first came up with the idea back in the Garden."

—Larry Osborne
Lead Pastor, North Coast Church
Bestselling author
Sticky Church* and *10 Dumb Things Smart Christians Believe

"Married couples could have no greater allies than David and Lisa Frisbie. Their writing has helped untold couples confront and overcome issues that would keep their marriages from being all they can be. As a person who is delighted to know them personally, I recommend their work wholeheartedly."

—Larry Morris
Adult Ministries Director
Sunday School and Discipleship Ministries International

"The Frisbies have a wonderful way of engaging their audience through storytelling. Their counseling ministry has tremendously impacted our pastoral team!"

—Joel Mullen
Missionary
Southeast Europe

"David and Lisa Frisbie are experienced, effective, and passionate marriage enrichment leaders. They not only write well about marriage; they live marriage well. Their insight is hewn from the rock of good practice. I highly endorse this wonderful new resource."

—Jesse Middendorf
General Superintendent
Church of the Nazarene

"As society continues its relentless assault on marriage, the Frisbies have responded with a positive way through. The focus of their ministry for many years has been to create marriage solutions through gifted writing and personal modeling."

—Paul G. Cunningham
General Superintendent Emeritus
Church of the Nazarene

"We've watched and respected David and Lisa's marriage for many years. He delivered our wedding sermon over three years ago and we still talk about it to this day. We suspect that reading this book will provide you with a similar experience."
—Christopher and Julie Rice

"It has been great to watch David and Lisa teach and instruct couples at our church. They have passionately communicated the love of Christ and have positively impacted many marriages."

—JD Larson
Pastor of Young Marrieds and Young Families
Vista, California

"When David and Lisa Frisbie write about marriage they do it with their hands, their minds, and a lot of other skills, but above all they do it with their hearts and their own experience."

—Rob and Ria Kegel
The Netherlands

"We personally know Dr. David and Lisa Frisbie and their anointed ministry for couples. Their lives and relationships as soul mates are the living examples in our generation. As professional authors and educators in this field of ministry, God has gifted both to become great blessings to us personally and our congregation. We recommend every book they publish!"

—Willie and Ellen Isip
Pastors
Living Rock Christian Church
Chula Vista, California

"Dr. and Mrs. Frisbie have had a profound impact on my life. Their ministry has directly affected decisions that my husband and I have made, and our family has grown closer to the Lord through their teaching and Christlike example of living. We heartily endorse them as servants of Christ, and as gifted and experienced ministers of His truth!"

—Mr. and Mrs. Nate Petty
Texas

"I am delighted to commend the work of Dr. David and Lisa Frisbie, who have a rich background working with Christian couples. They have learned to listen carefully, think insightfully, and write empathetically about marriage and family."

—Gerard Reed
Professor and author
Point Loma Nazarene University

"Dr. David and Lisa Frisbie's time–tested ministry has breathed new life into the families and marriages at our church. I would recommend their wise counsel, encouragement, and instruction to anyone looking for a deeper, more spiritually intimate marriage."

—Chris Foster
PhD Candidate
Nazarene Theological College
Manchester, United Kingdom

RIGHT
from the
START

a premarital guide for couples

by David and Lisa Frisbie

BEACON HILL PRESS
OF KANSAS CITY

ISBN 978-0-8341-2604-6

Printed in the
United States of America

Cover Design: Arthur Cherry
Inside Design: Sharon Page

Unless otherwise indicated, all Scripture quotations are from the *Holy Bible, New International Version*® (NIV®). Copyright © 1973, 1978, 1984 by Biblica, Inc.™ Used by permission of Zondervan. All rights reserved worldwide. www.zondervan.com.

Library of Congress Cataloging-in-Publication Data

Frisbie, David, 1955-
Right from the start : a premarital guide for couples / David and Lisa Frisbie.
 p. cm.
Includes bibliographical references.
ISBN 978-0-8341-2604-6 (pbk.)
 1. Marriage—Religious aspects—Christianity. 2. Young adults—Religious life. I. Frisbie, Lisa, 1956- II. Title.
 BV4529.2.F75 2011
 248.8'44—dc22

2011008184

10 9 8 7 6 5 4 3 2 1

CONTENTS

DEDICATION

We dedicate this book to Dr. Norman Bloom, who did our own premarital counseling during the winter of 1977 and the spring of 1978 then performed our wedding ceremony at a small interfaith chapel on the shore of Lake Koronis in Minnesota in May 1978. We've remained in contact with Dr. Bloom since that time, and he continues to minister and serve with the energy of a man half his age.

Across the years, Dr. Bloom has served his denomination in a variety of roles, including district superintendent. He has traveled widely and spoken to audiences of all ages and all sizes. One of the highlights of our long friendship with Dr. Bloom came as we attended commencement exercises at a university where Dr. Bloom was the featured speaker—on the fiftieth anniversary of his graduation from the university. What a privilege to listen as this gifted minister recounted five decades of service to his Lord.

Norman Bloom has survived the loss of two beloved wives, Margaret and Barbara. We knew and loved both of them. As we write this book, Dr. Bloom is doing well, active in ministry, still traveling to speak, teach, preach, and counsel. What an example to the generations that will follow him into Christian service!

We also dedicate our book to several key couples who have taught us about married life and the dynamics of making a relationship great. There are others besides these who have inspired and guided us, but space does not allow us to mention them all.

Paul and Connie Cunningham were our first pastors. Paul preached the sermons on Sunday and led a vibrant, growing congregation in Olathe, Kansas. Connie was our Sunday School teacher; she taught the young marrieds and we learned so much from her wise counsel. Both Paul and Connie have continued to impact our lives through our three decades of marriage and ministry. We have turned to them often for inspiration and direction, for counsel and advice. They have always modeled holiness and health for us. Today, their example continues to inspire us! Paul is now a general superintendent emeritus in his denomination. He is still actively preaching and serving, leading and giving wise counsel.

Gary and Juanita Jones were our youth ministers while Gary attended seminary. We were dating and getting engaged; then later we were joining our lives as one and becoming newlyweds. Gary and Juanita laughed often and led well; they were transparent and available. We learned so much from their example, and we gained so much through their friendship. We always looked forward to being guests in their home; we learned by watching the positive ways they related to each other. Gary and Juanita have served God in a variety of roles. They are now "retired" in Florida but still very active in ministry and still a compelling example of godly marriage. We value and cherish their advice and counsel, and we are still learning from them.

Hardy and Lucille Weathers were serving at our church when we got married and began our life together. Dr. Weathers served as the worship pastor—and much more. Spirit-filled and humble, he showed us how to lead congregational worship with a dependence on the Holy Spirit and sensitivity to what God was saying and doing in the moment. Away from the pulpit, both Hardy and Lucille were wise, friendly, and available to us as we learned about marriage and about life. They have remained friends throughout our journey of marriage and ministry. Dr. Weathers now serves as president of a Christian publishing house. We continue to find inspiration and direction from the wise words and godly lives of Hardy and Lucille.

Gerard Reed shared ministerial duties in our wedding ceremony. Prior to that time he had taught us philosophy and ethics in a variety of classes; both of us were and are in awe of his intellect and his voracious reading. Dr. Reed's wise and witty chapel sermons on relationships were highlights of our years together as college students. All who knew Gerard held him in the highest regard. We were honored when he agreed to travel to rural Minnesota in order to help officiate at our wedding ceremony.

After graduating from college we became friends with Gerard and his wife, Roberta. Both Gerard and Roberta were honest, extremely wise, and so helpful to anyone seeking advice and counsel about married life. When we moved west, we joined them for reunions of former students and professors, gathering at Big Bear Lake in the mountains of Southern California. It was our blessing to know this amazing couple across three decades until Roberta died of cancer.

After being a widower for several years, Dr. Reed was reconnected with a college sweetheart. Both had enjoyed long-term marriages; both were suddenly single. Gerard had lost his wife; Marilyn had survived the death of her husband. The two discovered a new love, half a century removed from their dating and courtship as college students! Graciously, Gerard asked us to share in his wedding ceremony to Marilyn, since he had originally shared in our wedding service. We joyfully agreed. The happy result was a sunset wedding on the beach in Oahu in January 2010. Two dozen friends and family gathered for a simple service that was infused with rich meaning. Young at heart and happily married, Gerard and Marilyn supplied us with profound wisdom and insight as we were writing this book. Gerard is himself an accomplished author with numerous books to his credit.

In our previous writings we have often credited both sets of our parents with being good examples to us. They are! Again in this book we want to express our deepest respect and gratitude to Lamont and Ruth Jacobson and Lee and Marilyn Frisbie for showing us what godly, committed marriage looks like.

Ruth and Lamont Jacobson, married for sixty-one years, are actively involved in their local church. And we do mean actively! Ruth is the worship leader for the congregation, choosing and leading music plus occasionally singing solos. Lamont has built, remodeled, and helped to plant churches. Both Mom and Dad honor their pastor(s) and support their church in all seasons. Their marriage inspires us and teaches us; their prayers and support empower our ministry at all times.

Lee and Marilyn Frisbie, married for fifty-nine years, are actively involved in their local church. Marilyn sings in the choir; Lee has taught Sunday School classes for teens, college students, and adults. He has led district-wide laymen's retreats and events. Lee is a long-term Bible quiz director and quizmaster. Both Mom and Dad continue to model outstanding churchmanship and loyalty to their pastoral leaders. Their constant encouragement and support sustain us in ministry.

These six couples are among many to whom we owe a great debt of gratitude. Although learn from books, classrooms, and academic environments, we tend to learn most from watching married couples live out the joys and challenges of doing life together, showing us God's love in action. When ideas wear flesh, we can understand them and begin to apply them in our own lives.

God knew this principle: He sent Christ to us in human form, to live out the life of discipleship. It was the best way we could possibly learn. In Christ we see God up-close and personal; we learn not only by His words but also by His example.

To the six couples we have just mentioned and to many others—our deepest thanks. If anyone catches a glimpse of God's wisdom in our own marriage and our own example, it is because we have learned from those who came before us.

We fall short of these mentors and teachers, but we keep striving.

We are still learning.

INTRODUCTION

Your XPR Profile

How Premarital Experiences Form and Shape the Contour of Your Life Together

Halfway through our first interview, Jenae grabs the baseball cap from her husband's head and plants it neatly on her own. She smoothly and swiftly pulls her hair through the cap's opening, ponytail-style.

She smiles at the result before Dustin even has time to respond.

"Hey," Jenae says to her spouse, looking right at him. "This hat looks a lot better on me than it does on you!"

Dustin reaches over as if to grab the hat back from her, but he's faking it. When he sees me watching him, the hatless husband offers this quick explanation for his sudden cowardice.

"Don't mess with her, man, she teaches kickboxing!"

Both of them laugh. We need the laughter.

We've been talking with this couple, both in their early twenties and married for less than a year, about the recent struggles in their relationship. They've both agreed to be interviewed for a new book we're writing, a book that stresses the importance of premarital experiences as you come together to form a new union.

"Man, I just didn't think it would be this hard," Dustin says, talking about his struggles to adjust to being not just a new roommate but also a godly husband.

His wife nods in agreement.

"Neither of us saw this coming," she adds. "We thought marriage was going to be a lot easier than trying to stay single and live a pure and holy life."

What surprised these two, both of whom grew up in church-going families and eventually met at a church youth camp, is how difficult it is to blend two completely different backgrounds into a unified idea of what a marriage should be. It's more difficult than you might expect to figure out how a couple ought to think, choose, and behave in their life together, especially since each one comes from a unique and different set of experiences and relationships.

Dustin, who tends to be highly rational and highly verbal, shares what he believes is the key element in the new couple's marital difficulties.

"We just didn't realize how vastly different our families were," Dustin says, looking me straight in the eyes to be sure I'm paying attention. "I mean, we both grew up in church, and our families have the same core values about God and faith and religion.

"I guess we both kind of thought we came from the same basic background, so becoming a couple wouldn't be any big deal," Dustin continues. "It's not like either one of us was marrying a nonbeliever or marrying someone from a different country or from a different race or culture. We thought we were the same kind of people, coming out of the same kind of families. It sure felt that way.

14

"This was supposed to be easy!" Dustin opines, continuing his narrative. "But it's been just the opposite of that. This is the hardest thing I've ever tried to do."

Once again Jenae, who is generally less talkative, nods in agreement as Dustin explains their predicament.

"Dating wasn't difficult, except for always trying to keep ourselves pure," she says. "But marriage has been one major struggle after another. Why didn't anybody tell us it would be this way? Why did I grow up believing that my early married years would be filled with nonstop romance and many hours of meaningful conversation with my husband each day?"

Jenae shrugs as she questions her previous understandings and beliefs. "When Dustin tells you this has been difficult, he's speaking for both of us," she reiterates. "Both of us have really had trouble making this relationship work."

What Jenae and Dustin are learning as they struggle to understand each other and form a new union is that every marriage begins as a union of two different cultures. Each family—even though it shares common characteristics such as ethnicity, economic status, religious affiliation or denomination with other families—is a culture within itself. Each family lives out and expresses its values within a completely different set of rules and expectations, history and experiences.

When it's time to get married, if we don't understand where we're coming from, it may prove extremely difficult to figure out where we're going. Especially if our families appear similar on the surface, we're likely to miss the landmines that may detonate later as we sort out money, sex, power, and other key issues. We discover that we each have deeply rooted feelings about the "right way" to do things, and we suddenly realize that the other person is coming from a "wrong" or misguided perspective.

So now what?

If we're like most newly married couples, we begin to bicker and argue, fighting to establish dominance and control so that our new marriage conforms to our preexisting ideas of what married life would be like.

I'm OK; You're Definitely Strange!

Later in the interview, we ask Jenae and Dustin to share some of the differences they've noticed between their two families of origin. It's a serious question, but we're quickly laughing as first Dustin, then Jenae, explains to us how crazy the other person's family is. Happily, both Dustin and Jenae are doing this in a good-natured way.

It isn't always this way when couples get behind closed doors in the office of a minister or counselor. Often, one or both partners can be tense, closed-off, frustrated, or already upset. It's a rare couple that can admit to problems while also laughing good-naturedly about the details. Defusing tension with inoffensive laughter and self-deprecating humor is a great skill for any couple to learn, young or old, newly married or lifelong partners.

As the writer of Proverbs told us long ago: Laughter is good medicine.

Today Jenae and Dustin are laughing; all of us are.

Dustin begins with an obvious difference in family values. "Jenae's family is hyper-affectionate physically," Dustin tells us with a grin, shrugging his shoulders. "I mean, I'm in favor of that between a man and his wife. Between a wife and a husband, I think affection is a very good thing! But in Jenae's family, everybody is kissing and hugging everybody else, and it's just plain weird! Sometimes the women kiss the other women, and the men kiss the other men!"

Jenae, who is not generally an interrupter, interrupts her husband here.

"Now don't go making my family sound strange!" Jenae says, laughing. "It's not like the guys in my family are making out with each other. My dad's parents are from Western Europe, and over there people tend to greet each other with kisses on the cheek. It isn't sexual, it's just friendly. Nothing more."

Dustin makes a wry grin. "Whatever," he says with an exaggerated sigh.

Jenae pokes him the ribs.

"My parents loved us kids, but they didn't display their love physically when we were growing up. They still don't. I'm not sure my dad has ever hugged me in my whole life," Dustin explains. "He loves me, and every once in a while he will say that to me with words, but you can bet he's never kissed me—not even once!"

"Well, then, he doesn't know what he's missing," Jenae interjects, and once again all of us share a moment of useful laughter. Dustin blushes and smiles at his bride before returning to our discussion.

"But you get the point, don't you?" Dustin asks rhetorically. "I mean, that's just one way to see it, but our two families are totally opposite in a lot of ways. And so the two of us are totally opposite in a lot of ways, and we didn't realize that while we were dating, planning the wedding, and starting to paint our new apartment."

Jenae rolls her eyes, saying nothing.

* * *

Before the paint dried, Dustin and Jenae were already beginning to realize they come from families with very different styles, ideas, and patterns. Counselors and therapists talk about the importance of our families of origin in shaping our understandings about marriage, especially about how a husband and wife should treat each other, relate to each other, and raise children.

Every family of origin is a unique starting point, and psychologists explain that our formative years occur very early—before school starts for most of us—when we're easily molded and when our brains learn and store new ideas with amazing capacity and resiliency. Our personalities, whether shaped by nature or nurture, tend to be visible and distinct, even in the first few years of our lives.

All of our premarriage experiences impact our later lives as marriage partners, yet the experiences within our own families of origin will carry a disproportionate amount of weight, for better or worse. What we've seen lived out in front of us as children is often what we'll reproduce in our own words, actions, values, and choices later in our adult lives.

And this is true even if we're doing our best not to repeat what we've seen, even if we're struggling to redefine ourselves as something completely different from the family we grew up in. As we'll see, the patterns we've witnessed while growing up are printed on us, hardwired into our circuitry, often at very deep levels.

If Dad tended to yell at Mom as we grew up, we grown-up men may yell at our own wives now, even though we promised ourselves we'd be different.

If Mom tended to withdraw from conflict and hide herself away in some quiet corner of the house, we grown-up women may tend to flee from stress or fighting, running away from confrontation with our spouses, hoping our problems will die down or go away without our direct involvement.

If we watched our parents argue, fight, and divorce while we were growing up, we may have decided that marriage is essentially pointless or that being married is simply a temporary and flexible agreement that can be canceled later by one or both parties after the "love" or "affection" has melted away like it always does.

Until we've sorted ourselves out pretty thoroughly, doing the hard work of reaching forward to maturity, we're likely to repeat the patterns, values, and relational styles we witnessed while growing up—even if we spent our childhoods disagreeing with those patterns and vowing to do things differently. The patterns we witness while coming of age will print themselves onto our conscious and unconscious memories, quietly directing our pathways, until we begin to deliberately and proactively choose our responses, values, and even emotions.

Until we are what we *choose*, we tend to be what we've *seen*.

More than One Family of Origin

There's yet another set of variables in play in addition to the original families that gave us life: any reformulated or blended families that emerged if our parents divorced or remarried during our childhood or adolescence. In twenty-first-century North America, each adult coming to marriage may have lived in two or three family units and family types while moving from birth to graduation from high school or college.

A typical progression might be for a child to be born to married parents, then live primarily with Mom (functionally a single mother) following a divorce, then live primarily with Mom and Stepdad following Mom's later remarriage. It's increasingly common for a child to grow up with multiple serial stepmoms or stepdads, as birth Mom and birth Dad marry, divorce, marry again, divorce again, and repeat the cycle.

A child might be born to a single mother, then live for an extended period of time with the birth mother and a longer-term boyfriend. The boyfriend never quite reaches the status of "dad" or "stepdad" yet is an enduring male presence within the household. Eventually the boyfriend leaves or is sent away, and the mom enters a short or long phase of single life and dating. New boyfriends enter the home, each staying for varying durations, and have some impact—positive or negative—on the growth and development of the children. These unmarried adults residing in the same household may never seek or accept any legal or financial responsibility for preexisting children. They may never marry the birth parent, adopt the child or children, nor form an official family. Yet to be sure, by residing in the same place and doing life together, these less-responsible and less-committed adults are shaping a child's ideas about marriage and family life.

Children in such settings—their number increases daily—live with a nearly permanent sense of insecurity and transition, waiting for a lasting affirmation and support that never arrives. They may cling tightly to one birth parent, deriving most of their worth and identity from that one relationship. Or, conversely, they may lash out in anger at that birth parent for "depriving them" of a "normal" family life.

Increasingly, when we talk about families of origin in the twenty-first century, we look beyond biological origins, and we refer to the multiple family types and the diverse family styles in which a child, adolescent, or adult has lived prior to entering the marriage being considered at present. The groom may bring his experience of two or three distinct families or family types into his new marriage; the bride may have lived through five or seven family types or seasons. Gone are the days when a typical bride had only one experience of a mother figure and one experience of a father figure who were married to each other before her birth and remain married to each other as she walks the aisle.

Where once a bride and a groom represented a sum total of two families of origin between them, today's bride and groom might jointly represent a dozen or so seasons of family life or varying family types.

Rather than mattering less, our families of origin matter even more when they are multiple and varied. It is extremely valuable to sit down with our prospective partner and unpack our experiences of marriage and family—preferably in the company of a skilled counselor—before we launch out into our new marriage.

Other Experiences Matter Too: My So-Called Life

Somewhat atypically among today's newlyweds, Dustin and Jenae came to marriage early, each having only one primary family of origin. Each went from home to college and, essentially, from college to marriage. Neither Jenae nor Dustin spent much time as single adults navigating the world of employment, responsibility, and relationships. Already dating seriously before their senior year of college began, Dustin and Jenae got engaged as seniors, planning a wedding three weeks after their shared graduation.

"What was I thinking?" Jenae asks now. "Wow! That was a lot of work, finishing up all my college courses plus planning a wedding. I should have waited until the end of the summer after graduation, or maybe even longer."

Instead, both Dustin and Jenae pretty much moved from their original family homes into similar college dorms and from those dorms to their first shared residence, an apartment in a fast-growing suburb of Atlanta. They brought fewer families of origin into their new union, and few experiences of living life solo, coming home to an empty house where laundry, home maintenance, car repair, and paying the bills waited for them—and only them—to show up and go on duty.

When adults marry at thirty—or fifty—they tend to bring adult experiences of family into their new relationship. So in addition to a family or many families of origin, these older brides and grooms bring personal experiences with adult family values—perhaps their own previous marriage or perhaps serious relationships that included cohabiting. Forming a marriage requires taking a serious look not only at the families that existed during childhood and the teen years but also at the nature and character of family-type experiences that these older adults have lived out.

In the pages that follow, we'll look at how your experiences of family life can shape your approach to the "big three" issues in marriage: money, sex, and power. We'll also explore how your previous history within a family can shape your understanding of how to live out your family life later, when you're heading a household. Finally, we'll explore the impact of your previous history on faith development and spiritual issues within your marriage.

Your XPT Profile

How Premarital Expectations Form and Shape the Contours of Your Life Together

Renee leans over and rests her head against her husband's shoulder. Lane, home on leave before deploying to West Germany, instinctively reaches his arm around his wife's right shoulder. A grateful wife smiles up into the face of the man she married. If Renee was a cat she'd be purring right now, delighted and content.

What a romantic ideal. These two look like a couple in love.

They are. But they're also a couple in counseling.

Married not yet eight full months, they've spent six of those months apart. Lane, a mechanic who repairs heavy equipment, has been serving his country, protecting his fellow soldiers by keeping their trucks, trailers, and weapons in good repair. Renee, a cute newlywed still in her late teens, has been living alone on a busy military base, sharing a noisy apartment complex with children and moms, pets and soccer balls, toys and tricycles. Every day has been a reminder of what she's missing: the simple joys of life in a loving family.

After spending so much time apart in these early months of their marriage, they could not wait to be back together. Both believed that their happy airport reunion would lead to nonstop romance and the full-on intimacy both had missed while Lane was away on assignment.

What actually happened was a surprise to both of them. After several hours in the bedroom, they emerged into a real life filled with fighting and arguing, getting on each other's nerves, and yelling at each other for no reason.

It's not the way they imagined their reunion—or their marriage—would be.

Welcome to Reality

While not all newlyweds face the unique challenges that confront military couples, almost all newlyweds face some kind of "day of awakening" a few months into their new union. It's a moment or a morning or a weekend when all of a sudden, one or both partners wakes up and wonders, *What have I gotten myself into?*

If you've been married a year or two, you already know what we're talking about.

If you're dating or engaged, this is something you need to realize in advance. The good news is, if you can sit down and work through some highly strategic conversations right now, you may be able to avoid most of the crash-and-burn conversations later.

We suggest you have those conversations now—and avoid those major arguments later. Keep reading, and you'll discover why most arguments happen and what to do about it.

Fighting with each other only six or eight months into your new union doesn't mean you married the wrong person or that your relationship is doomed. In fact, this kind of stress and conflict is typical in a new marriage.

If you're stressed out and fighting with each other all the time, take a moment to congratulate yourselves. You're entirely normal. What you're experiencing does not signal the end of romance, but it is, in a sense, the end of the honeymoon.

The first few months of living under the same roof are likely to be clouded by your idyllic and romantic visions about married life. You're together, you're finally out from under the authority of others, and the two of you can do what you want to do. You don't need anyone else's permission.

Together at last, you're doing marriage your way. Dining out a little too often or maybe way too much? Who can stop you? Staying up all night watching your favorite sci-fi shows on DVR? Who's business is that? It's your life. Finally.

Bonding and connecting sexually, energized and elated emotionally, opening presents and setting up an apartment and enjoying all the fun of playing house! There's enough adrenalin in these activities to sustain you for many weeks or maybe even quite a few months. For most newly married couples, life is better than before. At the very least it's a whole lot better than being two separate people, living in two separate places, dreaming of the day you could finally be together 24/7.

You're like a sailboat bobbing along above the surface of the waves. OK, there's some motion out here and the waves are high, but "Look, Mom, I'm floating! I may get splashed a little bit, but I'm not in danger of drowning."

Then all of a sudden, maybe six or eight months into a new marriage, the storm clouds start rolling in and the waves get bigger. Now the boat is tipping and stuff is spilling over the edges, and all of a sudden—you've got problems!

What's going on here? Like most people, you signed up for a pleasure cruise. You weren't expecting a sudden shipwreck; especially not now.

What's Wrong with This Picture?

Renee knew she was marrying a soldier. She's proud of her husband, and she freely admits to a common female stereotype: "I just love the way he looks in his uniform! He's so handsome!"

25

Renee also knew that her husband would be away on long deployments. With three years or so remaining on his contract, it's pretty much guaranteed that Lane will be away from home often and for lengthy periods of time.

Although Renee is lonely—much more lonely than she expected—being alone is not what surprised this young wife. Instead, what surprised her is what happens when she and her husband are finally on the same continent. After a day or two of being thrilled to be together, the two almost immediately begin fighting and bickering, quarreling over things that really don't matter.

It's depressing to Renee and frustrating to Lane also.

"This is not what I came home for," he says with a loud sigh. "I mean, for months I've been dreaming about finally coming home to my wife, and then I get home and all we do is fight! What's up with that? We argue about what show to watch or whether or not to go out to eat. Dumb stuff! It's not like we're fighting over big stuff." Lane is confused by what is happening.

Renee cries about it. "Maybe it's my fault," she says through tears that seem genuine. "Maybe I'm doing something wrong here. I want to do this better, but I don't know what I'm doing wrong. Help me!"

Both Lane and Renee look at the counselor, waiting for magic.

✳ ✳ ✳

A few miles up the coast another military couple is having a happy reunion after a long deployment. Married for ten years, this couple has three young children. The wife, who has a civilian job at a large church, is functionally a single parent. Most of the time, she is the only adult in the household.

With the husband finally home for a few weeks before deploying again, the couple has arranged for a weekend of low-cost child care, courtesy of good friends at church. They are making time for just the two of them a high priority. They considered checking into a local hotel, but decided they'd both enjoy being home together with no children around to take care of.

"I want Mack to be a great father to his kids," Amanda tells us with a smile. "But this weekend I want him all to myself! He can be a daddy later."

Mack smiles in agreement.

"I love my kids," he affirms. "But Amanda comes first. And who knows? If this weekend goes well, maybe we'll be adding to our family soon."

Amanda blushes and looks at the floor.

Mack and Amanda aren't going to fight or argue while he's home. They aren't worrying about priorities or solving problems such as how to stretch their two paychecks to cover the expenses of a growing family. After ten good years together and three separate reenlistments for Mack, this couple has learned to manage the peaks and valleys of military life, the long separations, and the moments of couple-time that are precious and few.

Arguing? Fighting? Not on the agenda, and definitely not right now. But it wasn't always this way.

"The first time Mack came home, we almost killed each other," Amanda says with a warm laugh. "I had a baby at home, and I literally couldn't wait for somebody else to finally take care of that baby! The minute Mack walked through the door I kind of shoved the baby in his face and said, 'Here, this is your kid! Take care of it!'"

Mack laughs, remembering the moment.

"That's pretty much exactly what she told me," he agrees. "I walk in the door after being gone for months, and she hands me poopy diapers and a crying kid. And I'm thinking—don't get me wrong, I love my kids—but I'm thinking, *This is not what I came home for! Park this kid with a babysitter and let's be alone together!*"

Amanda shakes her head.

"He's always the same," she says, pretending to be annoyed. "He always comes home wanting the same thing."

Mack reaches over and grabs the hand of his wife.

"You're right about that," he tells her.

Great Expectations

What Mack and Amanda realized very early in their marriage is that both of them had hugely different expectations for almost everything, but especially about how their rare moments together would be spent.

They had one big fight the first time Mack came home after being gone for a long time. Mack, who at that time planned to never, ever tackle a diaper problem, loudly told his wife who could deal with the poop. Amanda, never a shy person, promptly told her husband he could get back on the boat and sail away forever. Or words to that effect.

Then they looked at each other, and both melted.

"We both knew we had a problem," Amanda says now, knowing they have long since resolved their issues. "In that moment, without even saying anything out loud, both of us realized we needed to deal with this and find a way to make it work. If we didn't, maybe our marriage was over."

Mack nods in agreement. "I wasn't very flexible back then," he tells the counselor. "In the military, nobody asks you how you're feeling or what you'd prefer to do today. You give orders, and you get orders. Down the food chain, you salute and do what you're told. When people follow orders, everything works as it should.

"But marriage," Mack continues, sounding almost like a preacher, "marriage is not like the military. It's not supposed to be about giving orders or following orders or someone being in command. It's supposed to be mutually submitting to each other in love. For us, we each had to learn how to do that.

"Neither of us came into marriage knowing how to submit," Mack insists. "Not me, but not Amanda either. Both of us are strong-willed, and both of us knew how to dish it out and how to stand our ground."

It's Amanda's turn to agree.

"I'm a strong person, and I always have been," she tells the counselor. "But I didn't want to marry a weak man. I wanted someone who was as strong as I was, or even stronger. I wanted someone who could step up and take care of things. I didn't want to be a mother to my husband. I wanted to be a wife.

"So Mack is right, both of us kind of came into this thing with a lot of strength, but not much skill in making sacrifices or learning how to compromise."

Yelling at each other over the top of a newborn baby, Mack and Amanda realized their problem was their *expectations.* Amanda expected her husband to walk in the door and start taking care of a child he hardly knew. Mack expected to walk in the door and have his adoring wife jump into his arms.

What they needed was an expectations adjustment. For that to happen, they both needed to learn how to explore and express what they were expecting.

* * *

Mack and Amanda had a healthy and much-needed conversation within twenty-four hours of his first return home. By luck, or maybe with some divine help, they each had an Aha! moment at the same time. Each one of them intuitively realized that if they didn't sit down and work together, they'd waste Mack's time at home in a blur of fighting and yelling.

They called a time-out, phoned a babysitter, and literally went to the beach. Sitting there watching the waves, they flipped a coin to decide who would go first in spelling out their expectations of this brief opportunity to be together.

"Amanda won the coin toss," Mack remembers. "And since I was the one doing the tossing, I know it was fair."

"I wasn't very nice at that time," is how Amanda remembers her own words and her own behavior. "All this ugly stuff started gushing out of me at once. I was yelling at him for not taking care of the baby, not doing the feedings, not changing the diapers. I mean, how logical is that? He had been on another continent all that time! But I was telling him, very loudly, that I expected him to walk through that door and man up, be a father, and take care of his kid. I was loud and proud."

Mack interrupts briefly.

"I wasn't any better," he says quietly. "I sat there looking at the situation from my side—and only my side. I was feeling sorry for myself. I wanted Amanda to greet me at the door with nothing on her mind but meeting my needs.

"After all, I had been saving myself for her all those months. Do you have any idea how it is with guys in the military, including overseas? Do you know how many bars there are, how many girls in those bars? I mean, there are the professional girls and there are the free girls, and that's just in the bars. You can't go anywhere without seeing all these women who want you.

"So I come home after being good, and forget about the baby, forget about real life, it's all about me!

"I was thinking about me, me, and me—in that order," Mack sighs.

"And that's exactly what I was doing too," says Amanda.

Sitting on the beach near Oceanside Harbor, Mack and Amanda each realized their own selfishness. Each realized their own unrealistic—and unexpressed—expectations of this short reunion and rare opportunity.

"Both of us talked," Mack remembers. "And then there was just this long silence, this really long silence, because both of us had said everything we wanted to say. We just sat there, maybe expecting that the other person would agree with us and then we'd start all over."

Amanda nods.

"We sat there a long time after our speeches," she smiles. "Maybe I was waiting for him to give in, or maybe he was waiting for me. All I know is, we sat there for a long time. The sun was going down, and it was kind of a chilly day at the beach, and after a long time Mack put his arm around me to shelter me from the breeze. He didn't say anything, he just put his arm around me."

Amanda gets emotional as she recalls the moment.

"He put his arm around me, and I distinctly remember thinking to myself: *Amanda, you are a big, stupid idiot! Your husband is finally home, and you're busy being selfish about it. Shut up and make love to your man, you fool!*"

31

Mack was reaching the same conclusions.

"I remember thinking, who cares?" Mack says quietly. "I remember thinking that my wife was beautiful, and I was the luckiest guy in the whole world. I was thinking that if I didn't shut up, I would mess up both our lives. I just wanted to hold her and watch the sun set and worry about life later."

Talk About It Now Rather than Fighting Later

The idea is a simple one. If you sit down right now and talk through your experiences and expectations about money, sex, and who's the boss, you can work through the kinds of issues that often explode later and shatter the peace and contentment of your new marriage. Instead of walking through a minefield, hoping you don't step on anything, you can defuse your tensions in advance by talking about what you hope for, dream about, and expect.

We'll explore money management, sex and intimacy, decision-making and control issues, family life and dynamics, and then also your spiritual life together.

As you're reading and thinking, as you're talking and listening, you may come up with other categories that need some discussion. Excellent! The more you can realize now, the less you will fight about later. And to put it simply: that's the whole idea of this book!

1
MONEY
*Your Premarriage **Experience** with Finances*

When Bill and Melinda Gates of Microsoft fame were dating and considering marriage, they did not come to us for premarital counseling. Same goes for Warren Buffet, the Oracle of Omaha. After carefully checking our records, we can also report that the entire Walton family—so far—has not come to us for counseling.

When we sit down with premarried couples, or couples in the early seasons of their married lives, we are almost always sitting down with "real people." That is, people for whom money is scarce, making a living is challenging, and setting up a new household is more difficult and more expensive than they expected.

Early marriage leads to early discovery: everything costs money!

"I had no idea," Kelly tells us, flashing a dazzling smile through perfect teeth. "My parents took care of everything I needed from childhood through college. I had great health care, an amazing dentist and orthodontist, and my wardrobe was always up-to-date and first class. Looking back, I have no idea how my mom and dad managed that. It's not like they're rich or anything!"

Husband Martin, sitting beside her in a crowded coffee and pastry shop where we are meeting, adds his comment to the mix. "Her parents are generous people, and they've both always had really good jobs. Kelly comes from a very blessed family."

Martin and Kelly have come to us because they're fighting about money a lot, and they're hoping we can help. Money—or more precisely the lack of it—is one of the key stress points of early married life. It's rare when two people come together in marriage having had precisely the same experiences with money.

We ask Martin and Kelly who's in charge of the money in their new marriage.

They look at each other in the same instant, framing exactly the same thought as they both ask us, smiling broadly, "What's money?"

All of us laugh out loud.

We're sipping coffee and noshing on muffin tops, which have fewer calories that a whole muffin and cost substantially less, as we tell Martin and Kelly that coffee-shop dates are favorites of ours. Both of us love coffee anyway, and coffee shops tend to offer casual, friendly, upscale surroundings.

Before we can explain how our dates work, Martin jumps in with a few quick thoughts of his own.

"See, that's what I'm talking about," Martin argues. "That's great for you two, you've been married a while and you're both working. But we could never afford to do that! By the time you spend four dollars each for two coffees, then maybe each of you has a bagel or something, before you know it, you've blown twenty dollars. And, I'm sorry, but we just don't have any extra twenty-dollar bills at our house!"

Money Issues Are Global and Universal

Across the ocean in The Netherlands, newlyweds Mark and Daphne discovered a similar reality as they married. Although today the couple is well-established and prospering, they didn't begin their marriage as wealthy persons.

"Most of our arguments in our early married life came from a rotten feeling we both had about our finances," Daphne explains. "Sometimes we were overdrawn and had to buy groceries only for that day instead of for the whole week."

Feeling poor and wishing for luxuries such as new CDs, new books, or maybe going out to see a movie, the couple discovered that financial stress sometimes caused them to lose sight of what really mattered. They realized that if they weren't careful they could lose their focus and possibly even their relationship. They made a conscious decision to value and cherish each other.

"For us, the financial part of our marriage wasn't smooth or simple at first," Daphne says, "but being together and being married felt great!"

So instead of letting their energy and their joy be worn away by financial stress, the couple chose to bond, connect with, and celebrate each other. For Mark and Daphne, financial stress lasted only for a season. Meanwhile, they took deliberate steps to help their marriage last for a lifetime.

Their example is helpful for all married couples, especially those who are still adjusting to each other in the first few months or years of married life.

The Thrifty Romantics: Our Four-Dollar Banquet

We're eager to explain our dates to Martin and Kelly.

Sitting back in her chair, taking a slow sip of her coffee, Lisa takes the lead.

"One of our helpful marriage traditions is something we call the four-dollar banquet," Lisa says with the wide smile she's famous for. "We set aside some personal time, often in midmorning or early in the evening, and we go to a coffee shop for a date.

"We've been doing this for almost ten years now," Lisa continues. "Here's what we do: We go to a coffee shop that also offers bakery items, and each of us orders a muffin top or we share a whole muffin. That's our food for the date. Then we each have coffee, and sometimes one of us will have just water, which is free.

"When we first started doing this, quite a few years ago now, our total at the cash register usually came to about $3.56 or $3.67, but we rounded up and started calling it our four-dollar banquet.

"We still enjoy those dates," Lisa continues, "although our total usually exceeds four dollars by a little bit. We still call it our four-dollar banquet. We sit together and talk with each other about our thoughts, dreams, worries, schedules. It's not like we're in a planning session or it's business-related; we just talk through what's going on. For us, especially now that we've done it for a while, we begin to relax when we leave the house for our dates. We know what's coming—inexpensive, relaxing, high-quality couple time for just the two of us, just to celebrate our marriage."

Martin and Kelly look at each other as Lisa explains the process.

Kelly states what they both seem to be thinking. "We could really use some time like that for our relationship," she says quietly. "That would be helpful."

Martin nods his head in agreement.

❋ ❋ ❋

Lisa resumes her narrative.

"We've talked to couples with no money at all, couples struggling to pay the rent and keep the cell phone bill paid, and even those couples have realized that they could find a few dollars once every two weeks or so to get away, sip some coffee, munch on a bakery treat, and catch up with each other. Even couples who claim they can't do it somehow manage to find those four dollars or so.

"In fact," Lisa adds almost as an afterthought, "we worked with one young couple in South Dakota that was fighting pretty much constantly about money and finances and spending. When we told them about how we did our four-dollar banquets, the husband really caught the vision. He told his wife, 'If we want to save our marriage, we can't afford *not* to do that.' So the couple began a brand-new tradition and started having their own dates. We saw them months later at a conference, and they came over and thanked us for showing them that a date-night experience doesn't have to be expensive."

Martin rubs his chin thoughtfully.

"Maybe you're right," he admits.

❋ ❋ ❋

Whether you're dating or engaged, or perhaps already in the early years of your marriage, you'll soon discover that each one of you brings somewhat different experiences of money and finances into your new union, especially when it comes to spending and saving. Your experiences with money will shape how you choose priorities, make decisions, and set up a household. Your choices and decisions regarding money, unless you've done a lot of strategic thinking and deliberate planning, will most likely reflect your previous experiences, at least in the beginning.

Without knowing it, you've already been shaped and molded into having certain opinions about money and how it ought to be used. Your economic values may be among the strongest values you hold. Yet you may never have stated them out loud, or even realized what they are. Then, suddenly you're married, and you find yourself fighting with someone whose financial priorities are vastly different from yours. You may find yourself arguing with someone whose money style—or pattern with money—seems impractical or irresponsible. You're angry and upset, thinking, *Surely this person I married should already realize the value of money! Right?*

✻ ✻ ✻

Dr. Danny Gales, a pastor and district leader in Canada and across North America, believes that making choices about money is one of the most difficult challenges a young couple confronts as they get married and form a household.

"Merging two different lives in the area of finances—both of you having different experiences with money and budgeting as well as the use of credit—may be the biggest challenge you will face together," Dr. Gales explains.

Having counseled with numerous couples both before and after their wedding ceremonies, Dr. Gales is uniquely qualified to make this observation. He has seen the complexity of bringing two different financial styles into a new household and trying to make it work while disagreeing about spending and financial priorities.

Time after time, young married couples fight and argue about money. Sometimes these arguments escalate into a constant state of tension that undermines the relational glue holding the couple together.

"All we do anymore is fight with each other, usually about money," a young wife tells us in suburban St. Paul, Minnesota. "Frankly, that's not what I thought marriage was going to be about!"

She shakes her head, admitting the obvious.

"Why did I think we were going to be rich?" she wonders aloud.

* * *

For their part, Martin and Kelly are under no such illusions.

"We knew it would be difficult to make this work financially," Martin tells us later in the interview. "What we didn't realize was how different our attitudes are about money and spending. And what we also didn't realize was how much we'd have to give up. Both of us grew up in middle-class homes, surrounded by a lot of luxury and convenience. We just kind of took that for granted.

"Then we got married, and we suddenly realized that luxury is expensive and convenience usually costs a lot more than inconvenience!"

Kelly echoes her husband's wisdom.

"I can't even set up a decent kitchen!" she exclaims. "I can't believe how often I reach for something, only to realize, *Oh yeah, I forgot, we don't own one of those.* That happens to me all the time when I'm cooking or baking."

Martin and Kelly's experience is typical of newlyweds in many countries and cultures. All around the world, as we travel to minister and speak, to listen and to counsel, we encounter young couples who are surprised to find their standard of living has declined—not increased—as a result of getting married.

"Maybe newlyweds are supposed to be poor," Martin wonders aloud. "Maybe that's just how it is. But at least for us, the problem is not just that we're poor but also that we can't agree on how to spend the little bit of money we actually have."

"We're coming from very different places when we think about money and how to use it," Kelly adds for emphasis.

What about you? What kind of financial decisions and choices did you observe as you were growing up? Did you watch your father or stepdad spend wildly on his personal "toys" only to hear your mother yell at him for being immature and selfish? Did you watch a parent lose his or her job at some point, with the result that your whole household suddenly became thrifty and changed its style of spending and choosing? Were you raised by a single mom who carefully managed every expense because there was never enough money to go around?

All of us come from somewhere, with regard to economic issues.

What has been your experience with money and finances?

More to the point, how have you been shaped by your own family of origin, your personal employment and job history, your use of student loans and credit cards, and your financial life as a single adult? In the remaining pages of this chapter we'll look at your premarriage experiences with money and finances, using key questions as starting points for your personal discussion and discovery.

You can respond to these questions on your own, separately, and then compare notes later. Or you can read the questions together, talking and sharing with each other as you read through the chapter. Whichever method you choose, be sure that you invest as much time and energy in listening to your partner as you do explaining your own history, background, and perspective.

Money XPR Discussion Questions

Here are some discussion questions to help you explore how and why your financial perspectives may be different from one another. Write out or talk through your answers as thoroughly as possible. The more deeply you can engage with these questions, the more learning and understanding can occur as a result.

1. As you think about the adults who raised you, did you see more than one style of managing money while you were growing up? If you had two adults in the home, did each of them share the same financial values or did each seem to have different views on money and spending? Thinking only about your growing-up experiences, which adult head of household (mom, dad, stepmom, stepdad, grandfather, grandmother) seemed to have the wisest and best view of money and how it should be used? Which adult—choose only one if at all possible—did you most respect with regard to money matters? Why?

2. Did your family experience hard times or financial stress while you were growing up? What are your childhood memories of a parent losing his or her job or being forced to go without much-needed items because you could not afford to buy them? Was financial stress the normal pattern for your family, or was it occasional and rare? What

are some of your earliest memories of financial stress as you became aware that there was not enough money in the household to meet the immediate needs? How did your parent(s) or family manage to cope with financial setbacks?

3. Was your family relatively affluent or wealthy as you were growing up? If so, did you realize it at the time? What did your family have as possessions or do together as a family that other families in your church, community, or area were not able to have or to do? Did you grow up feeling in any way privileged or having a higher status than others in your community or your church? If so, did you believe that this was because your parent(s) worked hard or were smarter than others? What are some of your earliest experiences as you became aware that your family was perhaps more affluent and successful than others around you? Did you ever feel guilty for the things you had, the vacations you took, the money you spent on clothes or computers or video games and such? Did other children or teens ever express jealousy of you or your lifestyle? How did this make you feel?

4. Do you remember watching your parent(s) sit down and make a household or family budget? If your parent(s) did prepare a budget, were you asked for your input in any categories? Did you get to voice an opinion about priorities for your family? Did you want to? Did one of your parents typically pay the bills for your household and, if so, did that parent have a pattern or a style, a place or a time, in which paying the bills was done? What are some of your earliest memories of becoming aware that life

cost money and that someone was paying the bill? As far as you could tell while you were growing up, did your parents run out of bills before they ran out of money, or did they usually seem to run out of money before they finished paying all the bills? How did you discover this? How did you know?

5. What are your earliest memories of watching a parent accept, obtain, or use a credit card? What do you remember your parent(s) telling you about credit and credit cards? Did your parent(s) warn you about credit, that it might become a trap that could lead to surprisingly high levels of debt? When did you become aware—if ever—that your parents owed money to credit card companies and that the amount of money might be substantial? Did your parents teach you to use credit only in emergencies? Is that how they used their own credit and credit cards? Do you ever remember your parents seeking or obtaining credit counseling or financial counseling? Did your parents ever attend a seminar on managing finances? Do you feel as if your experiences growing up provided excellent training in the proper use—and potential misuse—of credit and credit cards?

6. How old were you when you first heard the expression *FICO score*? Did you ever hear that expression, or at least a similar expression such as *credit rating* or *creditworthy* when you were growing up? Did you ever watch your parents attempt to qualify for a car loan or a home mortgage? Did you get to observe firsthand any aspect of that process? Do you recall whether that process was successfully completed? Did you realize as a child or a teen that

obtaining a home mortgage involved extensive amounts of paperwork, with someone—a bank or a lender—reviewing very private issues about your parents' personal history, employment, and use of money? Did your parents sign or cosign loans for you while you were growing up such as student loans or auto loans? To what extent, if any, were or are you personally responsible for those loans and debts?

7. How old were you when you filed income taxes for the first time? Did you do it yourself or did a parent do the math and paperwork for you? Did you hire a tax preparer or did you sit down with piles of receipts and canceled checks and do all the work yourself? When, if ever, did your tax return become complicated and difficult? Has it always been your experience that tax returns are a short-form and simple process? Has it been your pattern, as a working teen or working adult, to get money back from the government at tax time? If so, how much money is typical? If so, what has been your pattern for saving or spending that tax refund?

8. Did your parent(s) practice the biblical pattern of tithing their income to God's work or the church? When did you first hear the word *tithe* and what was your reaction to the idea? Did you grow up actively tithing your own income from babysitting or your first job at a fast-food restaurant, or did you believe that tithing was something for adults or parents, not for children and teens? Did your parent(s) tend to tithe only when they felt they could afford it or did they tithe in good times and bad times? When did you make up your own mind about

tithing? What did you decide to do about it when it was finally your own choice to make?

9. At what age did you open your first savings account? Do you remember the amount of your first deposit? Did you make regular and systematic deposits into a savings account as a child or teen, or was your saving—if any—more of a random and haphazard choice? What is the highest balance you ever personally reached in your own personal savings account? Do you remember someone teaching you the value of saving and the value of systematic saving as a habit and practice? Who told you about this? Did that person practice what he or she preached? Who is the best saver you know, and why do you consider that person to be a good saver?

10. When it was time for a big-ticket purchase such as a computer, a car, or something expensive that you personally needed or wanted, did your parent(s) require you to save up and contribute your own money, or did they purchase these expensive items for you? What is the first expensive item you ever purchased with your own money, money that you earned or saved all by yourself? What kinds of expensive items did your parent(s) purchase for you without requiring you to earn, save, or share in the purchase price? Did you grow up believing that your parents should be more generous with you, less generous with you, or did you believe that your parents were behaving just about right with regard to big-ticket items you wanted?

11. Do you remember the first time a friend or family member asked you for a loan? How did you respond to that

request? Do you remember the first time—if ever—
you asked a friend or family member for a loan? If you
asked for help, did you receive it? What were you taught
by your parents or by the adults in your life about asking for financial help when you needed it? Do you recall any time when your parents asked their own parents, friends, or relatives for money? Was their request
granted? Did you grow up watching relatives and friends
ask to borrow money from your parents? How did your
parents respond when someone asked them for a loan?
Who taught you about the etiquette involved in asking
for a loan or responding to a request for a loan?

12. What was your first job that actually paid money to you?
How old were you when someone hired you to babysit,
wash a car, cut a lawn, or do a similar chore? Did someone approach you about these tasks, or did you go out
seeking a paying job? What was your first real job that
involved a paycheck and tax withholding? Do you remember the amount of your first actual paycheck? What
did you do with the money from your first paycheck on
your first real job?

13. Thinking about all the people you personally know—
relatives, friends, coworkers, and others—who is the
wisest person you know with regard to money and money management? Why do you consider that person to be
wise? Have you ever asked him or her to teach you about
money or financial matters? Have you ever made a conscious and deliberate decision to pattern yourself after
that person? If so, in what way are you seeking to model
your behavior on that person's financial wisdom? Why is

that person a role model for you in terms of finances and money?

14. Years from now, how do you want to be remembered by your own children, family, coworkers, and friends? To what extent would you like to be remembered as someone who was consistently wise about money and successful at managing money? Whether or not you ever become rich, is it your goal to be remembered as someone who always managed money wisely and well?

As you work through these questions, separately or together, or as you come together in a pastor's or counselor's office to consider these topics, you'll begin to realize that your premarriage experiences with money have been deeply formative. Your values about money have been shaped by your families of origin, your own experiences of employment and work, and the extent to which you've been rich or poor, successful or troubled, dealing with surplus or somehow always late in making your payments to credit cards, utility companies, and others.

Talking about your experiences will help you realize how each one of you has arrived at your current thoughts and feelings about money. You'll begin to realize not just *how* you feel about spending and saving, but more importantly *why* you feel that way.

2
MONEY
*Your Premarriage **Expectations** About Finances*

Was Janelle raised as a princess?

She stares off into the distance for a moment, pondering the question. "Probably so," she admits reluctantly, with a shy smile.

"Definitely so!" claims Cory, her husband of nearly two years.

Janelle laughs and confesses, "Well, I did get pretty much whatever I wanted. There were four of us kids, but I was the only girl. My mom loved finally having a daughter, and my dad liked to spoil me whenever he was around. So between the two of them, maybe you could say I was a princess. I never really thought of myself that way."

"They bought you a Mustang for high school graduation!" Cory exclaims.

Janelle looks at her feet. "It wasn't brand-new," she sputters. "It was two years old."

Cory shakes his head in amazement. He is not convinced.

"Any girl who gets a Mustang for high school graduation is definitely a princess, no question about it," he explains to all of us. "Even if it's not brand-new."

Cory wrinkles his face with irony. "And believe me, that Mustang was just the tip of the iceberg, princess-wise. She got whatever she wanted when she was growing up—just because she wanted it."

Cory and Janelle are in our office for financial counseling. Their church is about to offer the popular Financial Peace University. It will launch as a weekend event and then become a series of classes. Although Cory and Janelle plan to attend the course, they have signed up for some marriage counseling first. These days, they are fighting about money on a regular basis.

"She spends so much money on clothes!" Cory says in frustration, forgetting to speak to his wife in the first person. "She has to have a new purse and new shoes with every outfit. So if she buys one thing, it turns into maybe three or four things. Then she buys something else, and that becomes another three or four things. It never ends, and we can't afford to keep living like this!"

Janelle looks angry. "Well, we somehow managed to afford that new computer you just bought," she says with an air of disdain. "I'm pretty sure your new computer cost a whole lot more than my shoes!"

The counselor calls a time out, so he can explain the rules again.

✳ ✳ ✳

Later in the same week, another young married couple seeks counseling for financial issues. Unlike Cory and Janelle, this young couple has maxed out all their credit cards: his, hers, and theirs. Married for slightly less than four years, they currently owe more than $30,000 on plastic alone. In addition, they're making payments on two newer automobiles. Both husband and wife are still paying off their student loans from college. Total of all their debt, which doesn't include a home mortgage because they can't buy a house: $100,000 plus.

"We're toast," says the young husband in absolute frustration. "We're here for marriage counseling, but I honestly don't see how it can help. We need a lawyer, not a counselor. The only way out of this is to file for bankruptcy and start over."

His wife interjects for a moment. "I'm really hoping we can avoid that," she tells her husband, looking at the counselor for affirmation. "I'm hoping we don't have to do something so extreme."

The young husband is not convinced.

"Believe me," he says, "I've run the numbers a hundred different times, and there's no way out of this thing. Our only option is bankruptcy. Hopefully we can file a Chapter 7 and not have to do a Chapter 13."

The room is silent for a moment.

"This is the most embarrassing thing I've ever said out loud, to anybody," he continues urgently. "I can't believe I've been so foolish and gotten us so deep into debt. But the only way I can see to get out of this mess is bankruptcy!"

Differing Expectations

Back in the office, we're working with Cory and Janelle. As a way of helping them understand their vastly different expectations about money and married life, we ask Cory a related question.

"Cory, what's the most surprising thing you've learned about money since you got married?"

Cory thinks about it for a moment. "I guess before we were married I thought both of us knew how to delay gratification. I guess I thought both of us would be more responsible and give more consideration to what things cost."

Janelle remains silent.

"I mean," Cory continues, "I really feel as if I'm the only one who carries the financial load around here. I feel that I'm the only one who worries about our income and our spending. I'm the only one who tries so hard to make everything work out. Maybe that's not fair, but I'm just telling you how I feel.

"It seems like Janelle goes shopping whenever she wants to, without thinking about what things will cost or whether we can afford it," Cory continues, again forgetting to speak *to* his wife instead of *about* her.

"I don't think my mom lived like that," Cory says firmly. "I think both of my parents were in agreement about money. I think both of them realized the importance of being able to actually afford what you buy!"

Janelle is still silent.

"That may be kind of true," she eventually says about Cory's perspective. "The truth is, I go shopping because I'm depressed. Somehow shopping always puts me into a better mood and kind of turns my day around.

"I never really thought about it before, but Cory may be kind of right about this whole thing. I don't stop and think about what purses or shoes cost. I definitely don't stand there at Nordstrom and do the math or worry about our income. I don't carry the load of worrying about our finances.

"But give me some credit, I'm not out there buying the really expensive stuff," she continues. "It's not like I'm buying designer this and expensive that. I try to look for good prices on things, and I even shop the clearance racks!

"But Cory may be right about what he said. I really don't worry about money. I go shopping to feel better, and to quit worrying. And it works for me," she concludes.

Beside her, Cory just shakes his head.

After a pause, we ask Janelle the same question we asked her husband a few moments earlier.

"Janelle, what's been the most surprising thing you've learned about money since you got married?"

Janelle seems puzzled by the question and takes her time framing a response.

"Money causes fights in a relationship," she finally says. "It makes people mad and they say things they don't mean. Cory and I fight all the time, and over what? A new pair of shoes? A purse? I don't understand how something like a purse can end up making two people so angry and so ready to fight with each other.

"Speaking just for me, I wish we'd get along better and quit arguing about money all the time. It stresses me out, and I don't like it."

Cory has no response to his wife's comments.

❅ ❅ ❅

Meanwhile, the other couple is answering similar questions as we work through their issues. The husband remains convinced that it is time to see a lawyer, not a minister or a counselor.

We ask the wife a simple question: "What did you expect your married life to be like in terms of money and finances?"

She thinks for a moment. "I guess the American dream," she says quietly. "I knew he and I would both be working. I saw us as upper middle class, double-income, no kids, making lots of money and having lots of nice things.

"We are sitting here in your office having a serious conversation about filing for bankruptcy, and I have to tell you, I still think of us that way! I still think of us as an upper middle class couple with lots of money. I mean, look at what Roger earns! Look at my salary! Between the two of us we earn six figures, not even counting bonus pay and holiday money and other perks.

"So you tell me, are we poor, or are we rich?

"In my mind, before we got married, I saw us having it all—good jobs, nice cars, big house, everything. And we've got all of that except for the house. We started out renting a townhouse, and we're still there. We just haven't managed to save up money for a down payment yet."

Her frustrated husband rolls his eyes and looks at the counselor. "She still doesn't get it," he insists.

Surprisingly though, the husband's answer is much the same when we raise the question with him.

"I thought we'd both work, earn a lot of money, and we'd both be upwardly mobile at least until we started having kids. I knew once we started having kids our money would be flying out the door in all directions. But honestly, I figured that as long as we didn't have kids, we'd be rich!"

His answer is not terribly dissimilar from that of his wife. Both of them had the expectation that their lifestyle would be upscale, their incomes would be large, and their financial life together would involve ever-increasing prosperity.

Both of them seem mystified that life worked out otherwise.

A long time later in the same session, we ask them a very basic question at the root of these issues.

"Before you were married, did you work on a budget together?"

The wife's blank stare answers our question completely.

The husband looks at the floor.

"It's something we know we really need to do," he says softly. "Maybe after we file bankruptcy and start over, we can work on a household budget. We've never done that. We thought that with two high incomes we wouldn't need to sweat the small stuff. But I guess maybe the small stuff adds up after a while."

Beside him, his wife is completely silent.

* * *

Looking for points of commonality between these two couples, we find one almost immediately. In both cases they made assumptions about how their financial lives would go after they got married. And in both cases, they did not express these assumptions to each other. Each person, husband and wife, simply went into marriage with a set of expectations about money and finances. Each couple got married without having a thorough, rational discussion about his and her expectations in the category of money and finances.

As marriage counselors, we can paraphrase the familiar refrain that "Money is the root of all evil." We'd put it this way: money is one of the core stressors for married couples, especially newlyweds. This was true as we counseled during seasons of global and national prosperity. This is especially true now during global economic adversity and recession.

Whether times are good or bad, whether one's national economy is booming or imploding, it's always timely and always appropriate for a couple to sit down and share their expectations about money and family life together.

Take the time to hear each other out completely. Take the time to learn from your partner's perspective, instead of insisting that he or she pay attention to yours. As you explore these issues, you may uncover key differences in how each one of you expects the future to play out regarding money. Talking about these differences now, calmly and rationally, can help you avoid irrational, emotion-based fighting later in your marriage.

Here are some topics to guide you in your discussion time together:

Your Money XPT Discussion

Here are some discussion questions to help you explore how and why your financial perspectives may be different from one another. Write out or talk through your answers as thoroughly as possible. The more deeply you can engage with these questions, the more deeply you can learn and understand each other.

1. Think about work and employment. Do you expect to work after you get married? Full time or part time? Do you expect to work throughout your married life or only for a certain length of time? Do you expect to work after you begin to have children? Do you hope to retire early, or do you see yourself working into your golden years? Now think about your partner with regard to the same questions. Do you see your partner working after the two of you get married? Full time or part time? For how long? Do you foresee a time when your partner could or should quit working? When would that be? Do you expect your partner to retire early or at least quit working before retirement age?

2. Think about checking accounts and savings accounts. Do you expect to have separate bank accounts after you get married? Do you expect that each one of you will have his or her own personal and secret money to do with as he or she wishes? Or do you expect all of your money to end up in one combined pile to which both of you have equal access? Do you expect one person to be the one who will pay bills and manage the money? Or do you expect that each person will manage his or her own money, plus contribute toward joint expenses such as housing and utilities?

3. Think about credit scores. Do each of you already have a credit score? Do you know your own credit score? Do you know your partner's credit score? Which person has the highest credit score, and why do you believe this is so? Do you already know what kind of FICO, or credit score, is required to get the best terms on an auto loan if you buy a car? Do you already know the credit score you'll need to qualify for a preferred mortgage from a reputable lender? Do you know what credit scores are required by national agencies such as FHA and others in order to back your mortgage?

4. Think about total levels of debt you will bring into your new household. Do you know, pretty much to the exact penny, how much money you owe and to whom? Did you remember to include loans from friends and family members that you are expected to repay? Do you know, within a pretty close range, exactly how much your partner owes in total outstanding debts, including to friends

and family members? Have you already added up the total of your combined debt, before you get married?

5. Let's think about credit cards. How many credit card accounts do you have at present that are open and in good standing? Have you personally ever been declined or turned down for a credit card? Have you personally ever chosen to cancel and pay off a credit account? Do you know if your partner has even been declined for a credit card? Do you know whether or not your partner has ever paid off a credit card or credit account? How many credit cards do you expect to have after you get married? How many joint credit cards will you carry on a regular basis as a married couple? What is the interest rate on the card you currently carry? How much do you pay, each and every month, on total combined interest on your credit card accounts? Are you making any progress at all in paying down the overall debt you owe on credit cards?

6. Think about tithing, especially the choice to tithe to your local church. Are you personally tithing to a local church? Are you tithing a certain percentage of your income? What percentage? Do you tithe from the gross amount of your income, or do you tithe on the take-home pay that you actually receive in your check or by direct deposit? After you are married, do you expect to tithe as a couple? If so, at what percentage? If so, do you expect to tithe on your gross or net income? Do you expect to tithe on unexpected income from gifts or bonuses, or is tithing something that only applies to regular income like your paycheck?

7. Think about giving to missionaries, helping the homeless, feeding the hungry, or other good causes. Are you personally involved in giving to good causes right now? Do you do so regularly, or are you more of an occasional giver? What is your partner's pattern with regard to this kind of giving? After you are married, do you expect to be regularly giving to good causes such as world missions, hunger, prison ministries, and similar charities? Why or why not? About how much do you expect to give on an annual basis?

8. Think about investments. Are you currently in the habit of making regular investments? Do you currently own property that you rent out in order to gain more income? After you are married, do you expect to establish a regular and systematic pattern of investing, or do you see investing as something that might happen if you have the money or only if there's a surplus? Would you be comfortable owning and renting out homes or condos as one way of earning income during your marriage? Why or why not?

9. Think about buying a house. Do you or your partner currently own a condo, townhouse, or single-family residence? Is it your goal to purchase and own a home after you get married? What is the price range of home that you hope to be purchasing soon? Do you already know what kind of income you'll need to earn in order to qualify for a home mortgage? Would you rather rent a nice, new apartment or own an older fixer-upper house that needs repairs and improvements in order to be more livable? Which is the better choice? If you decide to pur-

chase a home after you get married, do you expect to receive any help—maybe down payment money—from your parents or family members?

10. Suppose you are already married and one of you wants to buy something expensive such as a motorcycle, new computer, or fancy camera. Will the one who wants to make the purchase have to ask permission from the other partner? Is it OK for one partner to simply make a large purchase out of his or her income without asking the other person? Will you set a price limit on what one of you can buy without asking or telling the other partner? How often do you expect to be buying major items? How often do you expect to be buying major items that mostly benefit only one of you?

11. Answer this question as honestly as you possibly can, instead of just saying what might be expected: Would you rather be poor and very happily married or rich with issues or problems in your marriage relationship? Explain your choice. Listen carefully to your partner's choice without attacking him or her about the answer. Can you put a price on happiness? How high is the value of a great relationship? How high is the value of being wealthy or having many material possessions?

12. This will be the final assigned question for this section, although you're encouraged to talk about anything else that may have come up during your discussion of this topic. Here's the last question: if you lived your whole life as a happily married couple, yet always seemed to be poorer than your friends and less prosperous than other members of your family, would that be OK? How would

you feel at the end of your life if you experienced a truly happy marriage but never quite reached a level of being comfortable, let alone prosperous? Would you feel more like a failure or more like a success? Why? Explain your answer to your partner and listen patiently and carefully to your partner's answer also.

As you work through these questions, separately or together, or as you come together in a pastor's or counselor's office to consider these topics, you'll begin to realize that your premarriage expectations about money and finances may be very different from that of your partner. That's why you're talking about these things right now.

It is greatly to your advantage to explore these issues carefully, calmly, and openly right now, before marriage, rather than waiting until later when you are stressed out, fighting and arguing, and looking for a marriage counselor.

Talking through these issues will help you plan wisely for the future. Telling each other your expectations about money is hugely important. This is a conversation you really need to have —right from the start.

3
SEX

*Your Premarriage **Experience**
with Sexuality and Intimacy*

Married for less than six months, Aaron and Shelley were at first afraid to approach a counselor about their problem. Neither one of them felt comfortable talking with their current pastor, who had been Shelley's pastor throughout her childhood and teen years. Although both of them loved their church and greatly respected their pastor, the problems they were experiencing seemed too personal to share with the local church pastor who had such a long history with Shelley and her family.

With limited financial resources, the young couple was also afraid of the cost of seeking professional counseling. They knew it might reach $200 per session; they had both heard that at least $100 per session was common practice. This kind of cost seemed to put counseling completely out of the question. If the cost escalated after the first two or three sessions, the price was not realistic for them.

Their faith was an additional factor in the equation. Both Aaron and Shelley strongly believed that life's problems were best addressed from a spiritual framework rather than a secular one.

"We don't put our faith in psychology or in man's wisdom," Aaron volunteers in a recent meeting with us. "But we do believe in God's Word. We do believe that most of life's problems, maybe even all of them, can be solved with careful study of the Bible and its principles. So, even though we didn't want to talk with Shelley's lifelong pastor, we did hope to find someone who could help us from a biblical and spiritual point of view."

Aaron and Shelley's shyness and the concern about the cost kept them from seeking and finding counsel for several months. Meanwhile, the problem worsened, deepening a hurtful division in their new relationship. Finally, when it seemed like there was no place to turn, Aaron and Shelley attended a marriage conference at a large church in a neighboring community. While at the conference, they picked up some helpful books and also learned about a counseling center maintained by the larger church.

"The host church set out some nice brochures during the conference," Shelley remembers. "And the thing that most got our attention about their church counseling center, besides the fact that they talked about being biblical and scriptural in all they did, was the fact that the brochure mentioned a sliding scale for fees. If you couldn't afford their regular rates, the church was willing to scale down the costs to adjust to your level of income." Shelley smiles as she talks about it. "We were young and just starting out. We didn't have any money. So for us, finding out that the price of counseling could be adjusted to fit our financial circumstances made all the difference."

Within two weeks of attending the marriage conference, Aaron and Shelley were sitting in an office at the nearby church, seeking godly counsel and practical advice about a serious issue that was threatening their marriage. Pent-up emotions poured out of the young husband and wife as they described a problem that neither one of them had been expecting.

As you've probably guessed from the title of this chapter, Shelley and Aaron were having sexual problems. Specifically, to quote the way Aaron first framed the issue for a counselor, "Shelley is afraid of sex and doesn't want to do it."

Shelley did not entirely refute her husband's perspective. "It's not fear, exactly," Shelley began, somewhat hesitant to share. Then she reversed course and agreed with Aaron's perspective. "Well, maybe it is fear," she admitted. "But I would say it's really more like avoidance. Here I am, a newly married woman with a wonderful Christian husband, and I find myself avoiding sex whenever I can. I keep making up reasons why I can't be with him tonight or this afternoon or this morning, or whenever he's in the mood.

"All I've done is make excuses," Shelley sighs. "And the few times that I haven't made excuses, our sex hasn't been so great like we thought it would be. To be honest, I don't enjoy sex so far, and it just doesn't feel right to me. I mean, I know we're married, and I know it's OK in God's sight. But it doesn't feel right, and I just can't get past that. I don't know why." Shelley's voice trails off into silence.

Aaron stares at the counselor, needing answers.

✳ ✳ ✳

Eighteen hundred miles away in another city, another young couple faces a problem that seems similar on the surface. The wife, Rebecca, is clearly avoiding sex whenever possible. The husband, Marc, is perplexed, disappointed, and upset. In this case it's the husband who is driving the decision to seek counseling. The husband's frustration and anger have reached the boiling point.

"We never have sex at all!" is how Marc initially frames the issue as he sits down in the counseling office. "We're newlyweds, we're supposed to be having sex a lot, and the truth is, we never even have sex at all!"

Rebecca sits quietly beside her husband, head bowed. She appears to be blushing but says nothing while her husband is speaking. Her body language indicates that she is highly uncomfortable with this topic. It's clear that this is not a safe subject with her, not even in the privacy of a counselor or pastor's office.

Meanwhile, Rebecca's husband continues pouring out his frustration.

"I mean," Marc continues, trying to draw the counselor into agreement with his husbandly perspective, "don't most newlyweds have sex all the time? Isn't that the whole point of the first few years of marriage? I know that married couples cut back on sex later—I've heard jokes about that my whole life. But I really thought that these first few years of our married life would be about sex. And to be honest with you, that's not what's happening."

Marc suddenly realizes how ridiculous he must sound. He backs off, softening his voice. The young husband looks across the desk at the counselor, still hoping to enlist some sympathy for his plight.

"Look, we have a good marriage," Marc explains as the first session unfolds in a quiet office. "I love my wife, and she loves me. We're totally in love with each other, and we both know it. We're happy—except at night when we go to bed. Then, we end up getting in a big fight because I want sex, and she won't do it." Marc looks over at his wife, who avoids eye contact with him.

"I love her," Marc says, talking about Rebecca in the third person. "I really, really love her. So why am I not allowed to express that love physically? Why can't I show her how much I love her in the way I really want to?"

* * *

Two young couples, both solidly Christian in core values, both attending churches that are evangelical, progressive, and filled with biblical teaching. Two young couples, both recently married, both expressing and affirming mutual love and affection between husband and wife. Yet what unites these couples, who have never met each other, is a similar pattern of disconnection in the bedroom and a clear dissatisfaction with the sexual aspects of their relationship.

Counselors and ministers report an increasing number of younger couples raising sexual issues as problems.

"Once upon a time," a busy pastor confides as he is interviewed for this book, "couples with sexual tensions and sexual problems tended to be more middle-aged. Often the husband was hoping for more sex or better sex in the relationship, while the wife was ready to retire from sex and just be a mother to her children.

"Nowadays," the same pastor continues, "I'm seeing more and more young couples who appear to love each other at an emotional level, and who seem to have a strong spiritual connection, yet they have trouble sexually.

"How is it possible," the pastor asks, "that in such a sex-crazed environment and such a sexually charged atmosphere, young married couples can't find the satisfaction and mutual fulfillment that married couples used to discover in those first few years of being together? It seems as if we're moving backward instead of forward."

The Power of Untold Stories: How Our Sexual Histories Affect Us

In the two case studies you've just read about, young husbands wanted sex while young wives seemed to fear sexuality or avoided being sexual. In other cases, it may be the wife who is sexually eager while the husband seems to avoid physical intimacy with his new bride. What all of these situations have in common is a strong likelihood that a man or woman's sexual history is impacting his or her ability to consummate marriage with a healthy level of physical and sexual expression.

Simply put, our sexual histories have a high level of impact on our future behaviors, including our behavior within a godly, legitimate marriage relationship. Bringing deeply rooted feelings of guilt or shame into our new bedroom can cause us to feel inhibited about a natural and meaningful way that couples can and should connect with each other.

God designed our sexuality to not only help us reproduce and grow families but also to be the relational glue that bonds a man and a woman together in strong and intimate friendship. The purpose of sex is not only to make babies but also to help two previously disparate people share a new life, united by a physical bond that has metaphysical and spiritual implications.

As Genesis 2:24 explains quite clearly, "For this reason a man will leave his father and mother and be united to his wife, and they will become one flesh."

Christ, teaching His disciples about marriage and relationships, reaches back to this same passage in Genesis. Once a husband and wife have been joined together physically, Christ explains to His disciples, "So they are no longer two, but one. Therefore what God has joined together, let man not separate" (Matthew 19:6).

Throughout Scripture there is a clear understanding that sex has implications beyond the physical. The act of sex, even if consummated with a prostitute, as Paul said to the Corinthians, has the effect of joining two persons into one.

When we have experienced such a powerful act prior to marriage, we may bring a complex and troubling mix of emotions into our new union, a union we hope and pray will be blessed by God. Meanwhile, because our emotions and affections are complicated, our approach to sexuality—even married sexuality—may be similar to walking through a field that is riddled with landmines. We join hands and begin to walk together, yet before we know it, we are in dangerous territory.

Unpacking the Past for the Future's Sake

This chapter opened with Aaron and Shelley. While Aaron wanted sex and wanted to enjoy physical intimacy with his wife, Shelley found excuses to avoid being intimate with her husband. The problem escalated until the couple sought counseling at a large church in a nearby town where they could obtain anonymous but useful advice from a scriptural and spiritual perspective.

For this young couple, the primary issue was a troubling incident from Shelley's past. As simple as it seems in review, Shelley did not surface the issue until a third counseling session in the office of a minister and trained professional.

When the issue did surface, it surprised both the husband and the wife. Both believed they knew each other's dating history and relational history, yet both were surprised by an incident that Shelley had never discussed with anyone.

As the counselor raised gentle questions about previous sexual experiences, Shelley suddenly remembered an incident from her life in high school.

"I was, sort-of, raped," Shelley begins. The counseling office is extremely quiet as the young husband looks deeply at his wife, unsure of what she'll say next. The counselor is suddenly fascinated by a pencil on his desk, rolling it backward and forward, displaying attention by his body language and yet not looking directly at Shelley, not invading her privacy in this moment.

Shelley begins to tell the story of a good date gone bad, a Friday evening with a high school boyfriend who also attended her church. The two had a pattern of heavy petting, usually in his car, and matters had never gotten beyond their control. Yet one night, as Shelley now remembers in the safety of the counselor's office, things went farther than Shelley was willing to take them.

"He had taken my clothes off," Shelley is saying, "which was kind of normal for us by then. So he had all of his clothes on, and I had none of my clothes on, and we were sitting in his car out in a farm field, just outside of town.

"He was kissing me at first, but then he got all rough with his hands, and he started doing things to me." Shelley is trembling with emotion and her young husband instinctively reaches out to take her hand.

"It's OK, honey," Aaron tells her. "I'm right here. Whatever it is, let's just get it out in the open."

Shelley continues her narrative, describing various types of sexual invasions by her churchgoing boyfriend. None of these invasions constituted the technical definition of sexual intercourse.

Yet without question, Shelley was roughly and selfishly used by another person, a young male intent on his own gratification.

Seventeen years old at the time, as was her partner, Shelley does not remember feeling pleasure in that moment. Instead, what she remembers is believing that she had suddenly become contaminated, spoiled, and stained.

Shelley is crying.

"We . . . hadn't . . . done it," Shelley slowly explains. "In the back of my mind I knew we hadn't really had sex. But what happened was rough, and it hurt me, and most of all it ruined my sense of being a good person. Up until that night I felt like I was pretty much OK as a person. I had always felt like God loved me and I was being a good girl, growing up the way I was supposed to.

"After that night," Shelley cries softly, "I knew for sure God couldn't love me anymore, couldn't accept me anymore, because now I was contaminated. Even though we didn't have sex, I knew I wasn't a virgin. I knew that someday I'd get married and I would just be a big fake. I wouldn't be a real virgin. I wouldn't be the bride I always hoped to be on my wedding day."

Shelley dissolves into tears. Her husband holds her while she weeps.

The counseling session extended well past its scheduled time, as the young couple reestablished their love for each other, a love that has more than enough room to forgive a youthful mistake. Looking in from the outside, someone else might wonder that such a seemingly small incident has such a great power, years later, to interrupt and affect a godly marriage.

Yet if a youthful mistake has power over our emotions—and it does—what also has power is the redemptive love of a supportive friend, allowing us to confess something negative or shameful about our history while receiving affirmation and encouragement. Whether this friend is a sibling, a pastor, a counselor, or a potential or current life partner, the power of forgiveness can and does trump the power of repressed shame. Forgiveness deconstructs the prison in which our shame has trapped us for far too long.

Several hours later, Aaron expresses this truth better than a writer could.

"I love you so much more now that you've told me all this," Aaron is telling his wife. "I mean, I didn't think I could love you more, but I do."

He is holding his bride, who has stopped crying, but her eyes are still moist and reddened from her tears.

"Listen, honey, I don't care about that. I mean, I'm sorry that it happened to you, but it doesn't change anything about how I see you. Not anything! Do you understand what I'm saying to you? In my eyes, the fact that some stupid guy did that to you doesn't say anything at all about *you*—just about him."

Shelley looks at her husband, wanting to believe him but not yet certain. Aaron manages to disarm the moment with sudden humor. "Would you like me to kill him for you?" Aaron offers, smiling. "I mean, would that help? Because I would be glad to go kill him right now."

Shelley leans into her husband's embrace, welcoming the healing power of laughter. Husband and wife relax and laugh together, releasing the tensions of several hours in a small office.

"It's OK," Shelley tells Aaron with a wry smile. "He's been divorced twice already, and he's the same age I am. I think he's miserable enough already."

A few moments later a young husband and his young wife are embracing. Enough trust has been built between the counselor and the couple that the counselor, also, is ready to attempt some humor in the moment.

Looking across his desk at the couple's sudden signs of affection, the counselor makes eye contact with Aaron and simply says, "Get a room."

Everyone laughs.

But it's the young husband who has the last word. Aaron turns toward the counselor. "I like how you think."

✳ ✳ ✳

Marc and Rebecca's problem is also rooted in the past. Once again, it's the bride's past that holds the key to her reluctance. Yet here the issue is not about sexual expression—even involuntary—but instead about Rebecca's beliefs.

Well into a second session with a trained counselor, Rebecca is finally able to verbalize the issue as she sees it.

"For my entire life I've been told that sex is dirty and evil and bad," Rebecca says quietly. "And then, kind of as an afterthought, I've been told that this dirty, evil, bad thing is suddenly OK if you're married.

"I've always wondered how that can be. If it really is evil and bad, what makes it different if you say some words in a church? How does that take an act that is something evil and suddenly make it all good and OK?" She shakes her head slowly.

"I haven't ever said this out loud before," Rebecca tells her husband, "but the truth is that I grew up kind of hating sex and wishing I could live my whole life without having to deal with it. And I know how stupid it sounds, but I grew up believing that my mom and my dad never really had sex. I know that's stupid! I mean, I know I got here somehow. But truly, growing up in my house I was absolutely convinced that my mother and my father never had sex: Not at all."

As the story unfolds in future sessions, Rebecca confesses that her mother, from the earliest moments of Rebecca's childhood, trained Rebecca to think of sex as negative, evil, bad—something to fear and to flee from. Rebecca's mother implanted this message so completely that Rebecca came to believe it and stayed far away from sex and sexuality, even when around males in a dating environment.

"I never did anything on a date," is Rebecca's description of her own sexual history. "And I mean not anything!" Every once in a while I would let a boy kiss me. But if his hands went anywhere, the relationship was over."

Rebecca brought a fear of sex—even revulsion toward it—into her marriage. And because a kindly but untrained minister didn't wish to talk about sexual matters, Rebecca and Marc's premarital counseling didn't explore any aspect of the couple's previous sexual experiences.

"Our pastor didn't want to talk about the sex part," is how Marc remembers the three sessions of premarital counseling. "He told us there were some good books out there if we ever had any questions, and that was the entire extent of our sexual counseling before we got married.

"Honestly, when he said that, I wanted to ask him to name a few of those books," Marc remembers. "But he seemed so uncomfortable with the whole topic that I decided not to ask any questions. I suppose you hear this a lot, but I was embarrassed to walk into a bookstore, especially to walk into a *Christian* bookstore, and ask them where all the sex books were."

Marc's comment draws a laugh from a previously tense Rebecca.

"That *would* be funny," she agrees. "Can you imagine walking up to a Christian bookstore lady and asking her where the sex aisle is?"

Marc and Rebecca laugh out loud.

Perhaps with the best of intentions, hoping to keep her daughter safe and virtuous, Rebecca's mother raised her daughter to fear, flee, and avoid sex. On the plus side, this rigorist attitude produced a woman who was, in every sense of the word, a virgin on her wedding day. In an era when fewer and fewer virgins walk the wedding aisle, this mother's training might be considered commendable.

The deeper issue, however, is that Rebecca's mom formed and shaped her daughter's imagination, emotions, and understanding of sex. The ideas that formed in Rebecca were not wholesome and healthy, because they were fraught with fear and supercharged with negative energy. Lacking any sexual experience whatsoever, Rebecca nonetheless believed that sex was inherently evil. On a deep, subconscious level, Rebecca believed that the path of virtue was to avoid sex altogether, just to be safe.

Rebecca's attitudes toward sex were formed in early childhood and reinforced throughout her adolescence and early adulthood. Walking down a candlelit aisle strewn with rose petals does absolutely nothing to counteract the power of a lifetime of cautionary, emotionally-charged advice about the harm and danger of sex. Getting married changed nothing for Rebecca, except that now it was likely that the evil of sex would finally take its toll on this "formerly virtuous" young woman.

Rebecca entered marriage afraid, reviling all sex as evil. Recognizing the depth of the challenges here, a trained counselor and minister decided to refer the couple for more specialized counseling. With access to wise counseling, Rebecca gradually processed her emotions, thought deeply about matters of sex and sexuality, and became a loving wife who could express her love for her husband in a sexual way. This transition was gradual and occurred over a period of time; nothing was simple or immediate.

✻ ✻ ✻

While these two cases seem similar—husband wants sex, wife wants to avoid sex—the reality is that sexual conflicts and difficulties vary greatly in nature and character. What's paramount is that for each person entering a marriage, his or her previous sexual experience will play a large part in determining how the sexual aspects of marriage progress and proceed.

Along with money, power, faith, and the other topics covered in this book, it is critically important that a young couple discuss their sexual histories with each other as part of the courtship and premarital counseling process. Too often, one or both adults minimize their previous histories, both relationally and sexually, keeping a positive attitude and believing that sex "will work itself out" in the new union. Too often the landmines begin exploding as the couple walks together toward a physical and sexual expression of marital intimacy.

The topics of discussion listed below are intended to help you as a couple, so that each one of you can discuss your sexual experience or lack of it with your future partner. Among other values, developing this kind of intimacy in your friendship and conversation before you're married will help you establish patterns of transparency and honesty, intimacy and trust, in your married life.

Sex XPR Discussion Questions

1. Do you remember your first attitudes about sex and sexuality as you were growing up? Was it a forbidden subject that you weren't supposed to think about and definitely not become involved in? How did you first receive accurate information on how babies are made? Who told you or taught you? Did you have sex education in a school setting, at home or church, or in any other formal way? If so, did you actually learn anything from this process? What do you remember about your attitudes toward sex and sexuality when you were a child and teen?

2. When you began to date, how did you establish boundaries to sexual behavior? Were those boundaries successful in maintaining your own sexual standards and values? Why or why not? If you were advising a young teen today, based on your own experience and your own actual behavior, how might you advise that teenager to keep himself or herself pure in a world that is constantly bombarding us with sexually charged images and ideas?

3. As a teenager and young adult, did you struggle to maintain your personal sexual purity? Were you generally victorious in this struggle, or did you often feel as if you were failing the purity test? How did you feel about yourself, especially in your later teen years, with regard to purity and staying chaste? Did you see yourself as a righteous

person or as damaged goods? Do your best to remember your actual thoughts and feelings, especially from your later teen years, as you dated and had serious relationships with others.

4. Have you at any time gone beyond a sexual boundary that you believe you should have kept? What do you think is involved in one losing his or her virginity, and would you say that you kept or lost your personal purity? As you prepare for your upcoming marriage, or as you deal with your early years of being together, do you regard yourself as a virgin until your wedding, or do you regard yourself as being sexually experienced before walking the aisle? Explain the reasoning behind your answer.

5. As you were growing up, did you have a healthy role model—perhaps a married couple—that displayed for you how a husband and wife should behave toward each other physically? Did you watch a romantic, playful, married couple and make the assumption that their sex life was vital and fulfilling to both? Did a married person tell you that his or her sex life was positive and wonderful, expressing joy and appreciation for this fact? Or perhaps the opposite was true. Was there a married person—perhaps an older sister or brother, relative, or friend—who confided in you about his or her disappointment with sex, frustration with sexual matters, or sexual problems in his or her marriage?

6. When you were growing up, what was your experience with pornography, if any? When did you first become aware that certain magazines, books, movies, Web sites, and so forth, were pornographic and contained visual

images of sex and sexuality? As you learned about these things, were you drawn to them in any way, or did you totally want to run in the opposite direction? Was there a time or a season in your life when pornography was a frequent part of your experience? Did you turn to pornography as an antidote for being lonely or to protect yourself from the desire to have sex with others?

7. In our current culture, many marriages are ending, some after ten or more years, because one partner has "suddenly realized" that he or she is drawn to homosexual acts and behavior. Do you personally know of a marriage that has ended or a family that has been torn apart by this type of revelation occurring after a fairly long and seemingly typical marriage? How did you feel when you learned about it? What was your reaction?

8. Our sex drive is a strong and powerful force, often shaped by our first experiences or our first awareness of sex and sexual things. Has there been a time in your life when you felt sexually attracted to persons of the same sex? How did you react and respond to these feelings, if any? Are you now, in any way, attracted to persons of the same sex? To what extent in your entire life up to this moment have you acted on a desire to be sexually involved with someone of the same sex? Do you believe that a person's specific sexual preferences are genetically programmed at birth, or do you believe that a person's sexual identity often emerges as a result of his or her formative experiences, especially early experiences, with sex and sexuality?

4
SEX

*Your Premarriage **Expectations** About Sexuality and Intimacy*

As Brooke and Richard walk into the counselor's office, Richard is visibly nervous. His body language says that he is anxious and upset, uncomfortable with the situation, and afraid of what may be about to happen.

It's not abnormal for a husband to be reluctant about counseling. It has been our experience the wife is more likely than the husband to take the lead in seeking counseling, finding an available counselor, making the appointment, and then following through with the sessions. Husbands often play a more passive role, in part because husbands tend to minimize or downplay marital problems.

Richard's anxiety, though, appears to be operating at a higher level. Richard is certainly tense. He can't stand still or stay in one place as he and his wife wait for their appointment to begin; he can't sit quietly once they are in the counselor's office. Richard twitches and rearranges his clothes and changes position in his seat almost constantly.

His physical markers indicate that he fears being identified as the problem during the session. As things develop, his fear turns out to be entirely justified.

The Abandoned Bride

"Here's why we made this appointment," Brooke says calmly after the counselor's prayer to begin the session. "We made this appointment because we are not having sex, and we are not having sex because my husband apparently doesn't find me attractive enough or exciting enough or something like that. Apparently I just don't interest him."

Richard squirms and fidgets but says nothing.

"Every night it's the same routine," Brooke continues. "We have dinner and watch some television, and then it gets to be close to our bedtime. I start getting ready for bed, and sometimes—can I be honest here?—sometimes I dress up in my sexiest underwear or my sheerest nightgown. Sometimes I wear nothing at all! I start parading around the house, trying to get my husband's attention. I just want him to notice me. I just want him to want me!

"We've been married eleven months," Brooke continues, "not even a year yet. But pretty much from the very start of the marriage, this is how it goes for us. Around bedtime I do my best to look attractive and be attractive and kind of set the mood, if you know what I mean. And it's like he doesn't see me or doesn't care.

"Am I unattractive or ugly?" Brooke asks the counselor.

The counselor treats this as a rhetorical question, declining to answer. Brooke resumes her narrative without demanding any specific response from the trained professional across the desk.

"I get dressed in something sexy, or maybe even nothing at all, and I do my best to get my husband's attention, but nothing happens."

Brooke pauses in the midst of her story, and the room is eerily quiet. Richard shifts in his chair, looks at the floor, and coughs lightly.

The counselor waits, his manner indicating openness and readiness. After a moment or two, the counselor takes the initiative.

"So, if your husband doesn't chase after you sexually, what does happen each evening?" the counselor inquires. "Do you both go to bed at the same time, or does one of you stay up later? Do you argue or fight at bedtime, or is it more that you ignore each other?"

Looking directly at Brooke, the counselor questions her directly.

"How do you react when your husband ignores you? What do you say or do? What kind of attitude do you take if your husband isn't paying attention? And if you're not getting his attention, where is his attention going? What are you competing with, or do you know?"

Richard looks at his wife, waiting to hear how she will respond. It's the first time during this session that his body ceased twitching or flexing or moving.

Brooke has an answer ready, but she looks at her husband before she speaks. She seems to be weighing how much to say or at least how to say it.

"I know exactly what I'm competing with," Brooke says in a quiet, even-toned voice with little trace of emotion. "It's called World of Warcraft, and it's some kind of online video game. He plays it every single night of his life and often during the day. I don't know if he plays it at school, but I'd guess he probably does. It's a video game—it's not even real—but it seems to be his entire life."

Brooke speaks calmly, choosing her words with deliberation. "I don't know what it means yet," she says slowly, "but I'm married to a man who would rather kill fake aliens on a tiny screen than make love to a sexy woman in his own bedroom. It's like he doesn't even know I exist."

Her voice drops to a whisper. "If I was fat or ugly or unattractive, maybe I could understand, but I take care of myself. I work out, and everybody tells me I've got a nice figure, and I'm in good shape.

"I think I'm at least as sexy as most wives, maybe a little above average," is how Brooke assesses her appearance. "I think most men would want me. I don't think I'd have to parade around all night in front of most men to get their attention. I don't think most men would rather shoot fake aliens than sleep with me."

Brooke looks at Richard, assessing his mood and response. We're well into the session, and except for brief introductions before the opening prayer, Richard has not yet said a word.

The Video Game Generation

We are marriage counselors who do a brisk and steady business these days with young married couples who are not having sex. It's a huge change from earlier days and previous generations when young husbands seemed to be supercharged sexually and young wives often wanted a little relief from their bedroom "duties."

At a recent marriage event for younger couples—mostly in their twenties with a light sprinkling of thirty-somethings—we asked the husbands to indicate by a show of hands if they often played online video games during the evening or late into the night. Almost every hand that was attached to a man shot up immediately, and there was widespread laughter. We noticed it was the husbands who were doing the laughing.

The wives were looking at each other in disbelief. Each wife had believed that her situation was unique; her husband was rare. Instead, as the show of hands demonstrated, we are witnessing a generational pattern that is taking wives by surprise and catching them unprepared.

For the first time in our counseling careers, we're working with young married couples who are in our office because from the wife's perspective their sex lives are insufficient or nonexistent because of competition for the husband's attentions. Not competition from other women or pornography, but from online video games that involve simulated fighting, killing, and winning.

Tapping deeply into primal male archetypes of dominance and conquest, competition and warfare, game designers have developed realistic simulations of intergalactic travel, interspecies warfare, zombie killing, and good old-fashioned soldiers on a battlefield. Early games were surprisingly popular even without the advances in animation and computerized graphics that today's games feature.

An entire generation of males is coming of age with joysticks in their hands, spraying bullets at zombies, and talking trash with teenagers in faraway states—night after night after night. They stare into their computer screens long after they should be in bed, taking little thought of the work, study, or other chores of tomorrow.

Their wives are becoming somewhat of a stereotype among newly-married twenty-something couples. And although pornography is a genuine issue, as we'll discuss in the case that follows, a substantial number of husbands are engaged, not in viewing pornography, but in shedding vicarious blood and killing anonymous androids, often as part of competitive teams.

"I think these kinds of games are porn too, but of a different type," says one frustrated wife, age twenty-four. "Violence is porn, warfare is porn," she continues.

We'll leave that specific question and topic to other books and other experts. Meanwhile we'll simply comment on what we observe daily in the field of marriage counseling. Young husbands are staying away from their bedrooms and their wives in order to shoot, stab, maim, and kill imaginary opponents.

The New "Other Woman"

A few hundred miles away, we work with another young couple that is not having sex very often. Once again, it's the wife who comes to us with the primary complaint. How different from the days when men seemed to badger, whine, and cajole their wives into having sex!

We're less than ten minutes into our first session with this couple when the wife tells us exactly what is going on in their home.

"He'd been ignoring me almost from the honeymoon," she says flatly and with some edges of malice in her voice. "He wasn't acting much like a husband. He wasn't looking at me or giving me compliments. We had sex a few times on our honeymoon, but it was way less than I was expecting. At the time, I thought maybe he was just tired or worn out from all the wedding stuff. Both of us were exhausted when the honeymoon started."

She pauses before continuing with her narrative. "Anyway, we moved into our new apartment and we bought this big beautiful bed with a great mattress. It seemed like a perfect love nest for us, and even the bed itself was romantic and big and inviting and comfortable.

"I couldn't wait to try it out! But night after night, my husband wouldn't go to bed with me. He'd tell me to go bed, and then he'd make up some story about how he had to stay up late to do some project for the office.

"I remember being kind of surprised that he had so much work to take home with him every day," she says quietly. "And I very quickly became aware that he wasn't exactly chasing me around the bed."

Both husband and wife are silent for a moment.

"So anyway," the wife resumes, "about two weeks ago I came out into the living room about 3 A.M. and there he was, staring at a computer screen, and it wasn't exactly work from the office."

She struggles to find her voice. "He didn't know I was awake, and he didn't notice that I came into the room," she says in a whisper. "I couldn't tell what was happening at first. But when I got closer I noticed that he was . . ."

Her husband quickly interrupts. "I'm sure he can figure out what I was doing! I don't think you need to explain it to him."

The room goes quiet and stays quiet.

In this case, the young husband was not an online video gamer. Instead, he was a newly married male addicted to pornographic images of a certain type, images that aroused his passion and stirred him to take specific actions in response. The patterns he formed as a college student and single person followed him into his married life, reinforcing their hold on his imagination and behavior.

In the counseling sessions that followed, it became extremely clear that this husband didn't fall short in his sex drive; he was having sex practically every night of his life. However, as the story itself makes clear, he wasn't involving his wife in the process. He was gratifying himself, all alone, while an attractive young woman waited longingly in the bedroom for a lover who never arrived.

Unfortunately, this wife's experience is also becoming more prevalent in today's society. In a world in which sex is increasingly viewed as an expression of personal pleasure aimed at gratifying one's own desires and preferences rather than joining another person in an expression of shared love and intimacy, men are increasingly abandoning their real-live wives in favor of sexual experiences in front of a television image or computer screen, with no other person directly involved.

Sex of this type is easily accessible and widely available. There are no performance issues or worries about comparisons. A male is not required to take into account whether his wife is receiving pleasure or experiencing joy. Instead, sex becomes yet another casual pursuit of the me generation, a way to have a moment of personal enjoyment in the midst of busy, stressed-out, angst-ridden lives.

Increasingly, the computer screen has replaced the other woman as an enticement for a husband to stray away from his marriage partner. The new affair is man plus screen, not man plus mistress. The screen is available 24/7, always ready and willing, and makes few demands of its addicted victims.

Wives, especially young wives, are traumatized to discover that the godly young man they married is entranced by images of anonymous naked women. These wives feel abandoned and betrayed, and also violated. They have entered into a relationship and a contract—marriage—and they had believed it would involve a mutual expression of physical and sexual love.

When this expression of love vanishes or becomes rare, wives worry that they've married a gay man or a nonsexual one. In most cases, the explanation is somewhat simpler. The young husband, having already established the behavioral pattern as an adolescent or a college student, is deeply involved in pornography, usually via the Internet, and is addicted to the sexual and chemical highs that interacting with pornography can provide.

The addictive cycle of gratification through pornography includes an adrenalin rush that is chemical and real. This rush may be stronger and more enticing than the endorphin response of sexual intercourse with a person. In candid and unguarded moments, young husbands have told us that sex alone is more fulfilling and more fun than sex with their wives, which is why they prefer it. Clearly these young males view sex as being about them, rather than a process of serving and giving, connecting and joining, growing together in love and affection with another human being. This is a deficient view of sex and sexuality.

Other writers have explained and documented the adrenalin cycle as one factor in the complex equation of male sexual selfishness and marital abandonment. In these pages we need not repeat this helpful information; we'll refer to it among the recommended resources we list for this section. What we'll note here is that the pleasure and joy of sex is part of God's design for combining two lives into one living organism, a new union that is spiritual, emotional, physical, and lifelong.

These good purposes are short-circuited when sex is seen as personal gratification, personal pleasure, and personal enjoyment. What is needed is to go on to maturity. As we mature, we learn that serving others, giving and receiving, caring about the person to whom you are committed, and behaviors such as these breathe life and health into ourselves, our families, and our communities.

We don't need more sex, less sex, or better sex; we need more maturity.

* * *

The purpose of this chapter is specific and immediate: to help a couple currently dating or engaged or even recently married to actively and proactively talk about their sexual expectations, aspirations, and behaviors. Doing so is absolutely crucial to the process of becoming intimate friends and lovers.

We have already explored, in the previous section, sexuality and the power and importance of our sexual histories. Now, in this chapter, we are looking forward—not backward. What do you expect about sexuality and intimacy, bonding and connecting, and being together in the bedroom as you begin your new life together?

The topics of discussion listed below are intended to help you as a couple so that each one of you can discuss your expectations and hopes in this category with your future partner. Expressing your thoughts clearly and honestly about these questions can help your partner better understand your perspective. Listening intently and well can help you better understand the person you are about to marry.

Your Sex XPT Discussion

1. Think back to the opening story about the young husband who was a video gamer earlier in this section. Did you recognize someone you know as you were reading that

story? Do you have any friends who seem to be addicted to online, competitive video games? Are some of those friends already married? How about you? Would you expect to spend more time online killing aliens than you spend in the bedroom, making love to your spouse? If you're a male, can you imagine hoping your wife will go to bed early so that you can have more time to yourself to play video games? If you're a wife, how would you feel if your husband cared more about gaming than he cared about you?

2. How would you counsel the young couple described in the first story of this chapter? What might you say to the young husband who spent many hours every night playing war? What might you say to the young wife who dressed up in sexy clothes, only to feel as if her husband didn't even see her? In your opinion, what is the way forward for this couple? How can they connect and grow together instead of falling apart? Is there any hope for this couple and, if so, where does this hope come from?

3. Have you talked with many married couples about their honeymoon experiences? Do you understand how some couples might be totally exhausted after all the wedding celebrations to the point that their wedding night is not actually such a big deal? Having said that, can you imagine a couple going on a honeymoon for a week or two and not having much sex? If you heard about a couple with that kind of experience—and both of them were healthy— what would you think about it? Do you personally assume and believe that a good honeymoon would have plenty of sex involved?

4. Will both of you be working after you get married? If so, can you imagine that one or both of you might be tired at times—so tired that maybe sex doesn't seem all that attractive? Is that kind of feeling or attitude normal, or should a healthy married adult be interested in sex most of the time? What do you think is "normal" for a newly married couple?

5. Have you talked with a married couple about the change(s) in their sexual relationship after they began to have children? If so, what did you learn from those conversations? Can you imagine how a young wife and mother might be so exhausted from childcare that she's not in the mood as often as she once was? Does this seem normal to you? In your opinion, should a wife who is not in the mood go along anyway as part of being a good wife? In your opinion, should a husband whose wife is not in the mood honor her physical and emotional state and postpone sex? How does love behave as a wife? How does love behave as a husband? How does serving one another work itself out in questions about having sex or not having sex when one of you is tired, stressed out, or simply not interested at that moment?

6. If you learned that a friend of yours was addicted to pornography, how might you respond? If your friend asked you for counsel or advice, what might you say? Do you believe that viewing and accessing pornography makes a person more loving and caring? Do you believe that viewing and accessing pornography teaches a person to be a wiser and more compassionate life partner? Increasingly, women are also viewing pornography, although addictive behaviors in

women appear to be less common. How does the use of pornography tend to impact a marriage and family?

7. Suppose your married sister came to you and told you that her husband was addicted to pornography. Suppose she was ready to leave him because of it. Would you advise her to stay in the relationship if the husband did not acknowledge pornography as a problem? Would you advise her to stay in the relationship if the husband insisted on continuing with his addiction? How would you counsel a wife whose husband insisted that pornography would always be a part of his life, no matter what? How should such a wife react?

8. Paul writes that a husband should not consider his body to be his own, but rather that it belongs to his wife. Paul writes that in the same way a wife should not consider her body to be her own but should consider that after marriage it belongs to her husband. Does this point of view seem extreme to you, or can you understand what Paul is saying here? Does this biblical counsel give us any insight as to how to respond to questions about Internet pornography and other such addictions? If so, how does Paul's wisdom from the first century A.D. impact this very contemporary issue we face today? If you were a married person, and you discovered that your partner was involved with pornography, how would you feel? What would you say to your partner about this topic? What kind of outcome or result would you hope for? Would you personally remain in a long-term, committed relationship with someone who insisted on remaining involved with pornography? Why or why not?

5
POWER

*Your Premarriage **Experience** with Power and Control*

Garrett grew up in Texas, but today he lives in an upscale suburb of Oklahoma City. He works in the oil business—his way of saying that he manages a busy gas station and convenience store located a few miles from his home.

Garrett and Cindy, married just over a year, have been thinking about going to marriage counseling almost since the day they got married. For Cindy, the clues were visible even on the honeymoon: a two-week trip to an all-inclusive resort in Mexico that caters to couples.

"We were right there in the middle of paradise," Cindy sighs as she recalls the honeymoon experience, "with pools and beaches and palm trees and tons of food service. Everything we needed was right there. And in the midst of that, the only thing my new husband wanted to do was play online video games!" On their honeymoon, Cindy couldn't pry Garrett away from the Wii. For her, that was a sign of trouble ahead.

Garrett and Cindy are sitting in the counselor's office, beginning to talk about the issues that divide them. Both are talkative, engaging, and social. Both are personally warm and friendly. At first glance, the couple does not seem troubled by any normal definition.

Yet early in their conversation, sharp differences emerge.

"I think we're doing pretty well overall," a confident Garrett says regarding their marriage. "I mean, a few months ago we survived a big pregnancy scare. Now *that* was a big deal! We are so not ready to have kids!"

Cindy interjects to disagree.

"I think a kid or two might be just what we need," she insists. "At least then I'd have somebody to share my life with. Right now my husband is either at work for sixty hours a week, or else at home staring at his computer and killing aliens instead of talking to me!"

Garrett looks at his wife and shakes his head.

"We've already been through this," he protests.

"And we didn't get anywhere," she retorts. "That's why we're here."

Typical Adjustments, or Signs of Trouble?

If Garrett and Cindy were simply having trouble making typical adjustments to being married, their story wouldn't be included in this book. Instead, as the couple shares their experiences with a counselor, it quickly becomes clear that the two are doing more than merely dealing with normal marital adjustments. These two are having their first major battle over who is in control. They are fighting over who holds the power in their relationship.

"Am I being unreasonable here?" Cindy asks the counselor early in their first session. "Am I wrong to think that a newly married husband ought to spend some time getting to know his wife? Am I wrong to think that he at least ought to be eager to go to bed with her at night? Is that so unreasonable?" Cindy is hoping that the counselor will quickly agree with her perspective.

Garrett jumps in immediately. "Before you answer that," Garrett instructs the counselor brashly, "ask her who brought her flowers, just last week, for no reason at all!"

Garrett is hoping to score some points with the counselor by appearing to be a romantic, caring, attentive husband.

Cindy is surprisingly ready for the flowers comment.

"You work at a convenience store!" Cindy exclaims. "You sell the flowers right there on the counter! It's not like you had to think about it or go somewhere or pay money to buy me a nice gift. You just scooped up some flowers from the counter and brought them home!"

Cindy glares at her husband, who is momentarily at a loss for words.

The counselor interjects to ask a nonthreatening question, and the tension is defused for the time being. What's evident is that roughly twelve months into their new union, this couple is already battling for control and power.

Later in the session, Garrett frames the issue the way he sees it. "Here's what I'm saying. I'm saying that it's my own business how I spend my time. I'm the husband here. I'm the man of the house, I'm the main support financially, and according to Scripture I'm also the leader of the family. Basically that means I'm the boss. So if I'm really the boss around here, why should I answer to somebody else about what I do with my time?

"That's the kind of question an employee should be answering, not a boss," Garrett continues. "At work I'm the manager of the store, and I sure don't have to explain my priorities or my time management to my employees. I don't work for them. They work for me! See the difference? And it's the same at home. Cindy may not be my employee, but let's get one thing really straight here, she is definitely not my boss."

With that, Garrett from Texas is done making big speeches. As far as he's concerned, there is one right answer for this problem, and he's just expressed it clearly for the benefit of all of us.

❋ ❋ ❋

Same Problem, Different City

Seven hundred miles away in scenic New Mexico, another young couple faces a similar issue from a different perspective. For this couple, it's not the husband who is charged with failing to invest in the relationship, it's the wife.

At least that's how the husband sees it. He pours out his heart in the office of a minister who is also a friend of the family.

"I never see her anymore," the husband laments, talking about his wife as if she was not even in the room. "All we do is work. When I finally come home from work, she's never there!"

Although the counselor continually reminds the husband to talk *to* his wife instead of *about* her, the young husband can't quite make the mental connection. He keeps talking about his wife as if she was somewhere else.

"I honestly saw her more often when we were still dating," the husband continues, ignoring yet another instruction from the counselor about how to express his thoughts and feelings.

The counselor interrupts again with a gentle reminder.

"Michael, you need to express that thought directly to Amy, instead of referring to her in the third person," the counselor observes. "Amy is right here with us. So instead of talking to me about her, talk to her about how you feel."

Michael nods his head.

"I saw you a lot more often when we were dating than I do now," Michael says as he looks toward his wife. She is sitting only a few feet away from him, yet by her body language she indicates separation, aloofness, and a guarded position.

Hearing Michael's direct comment, she frames her own response.

"That's just not true," Amy corrects her husband. "I'm home all the time, I'm around all the time, and I'm available all the time. You're making a big deal out of absolutely nothing. We're living together now, in the same apartment, and there's no way you're seeing less of me than you did before. Here we are talking to a counselor about our problems, and you're already wrong about what's going on!" Amy fumes with obvious frustration.

Michael sags in his chair. "I'm just telling you how it feels to me," he replies.

Married less than a year, Michael and Amy attend the church in which Amy grew up, a midsize community of faith in a mostly upscale suburb. Amy was baptized in this church as a child; she grew up here and knows almost everyone. Michael, who met his new wife at college, lacks connections here. He grew up in the Pacific Northwest and is still adapting to the dry desert climate and the cultural differences between the Oregon coast and the mountains of New Mexico.

As their first session unfolds, it's evident that Michael and Amy, like Garrett and Cindy, are working through issues of power and control. In many ways, their situations are similar, yet the roles are reversed. For Michael and Amy in New Mexico, it's the wife who seems to be the absentee partner. For Garrett and Cindy, it's the husband who's apparently not fully engaged in the relationship.

Michael continues his narrative, finally having learned how to express his thoughts and feelings directly to his wife.

"I like your friends, I really do," Michael says quietly, trying to win over his wife by kindness and a gentle demeanor. "I like all of them—well, maybe not Judy—but I like the rest of them."

Amy, still defensive in her tone and posture, actually grins as Michael mentions Judy. Michael sees the grin and is encouraged by it.

"It's not really about your friends, it's about how much time you spend with them and how often you do things with them and how little time you and I have to just be together as a couple," Michael explains. "That's what I'm talking about. I just wish you and I had more time together as a couple, and we could if you would spend less time with your girlfriends. You're out with them all the time!"

Amy considers this argument before replying. "So what you're saying is—you're jealous," Amy opines. She's taken a few psychology classes in school and she enjoys projecting underlying motives into the actions and behaviors of those around her.

Michael looks quizzical.

"I never thought of it that way," he begins.

"You're jealous," explains an emboldened Amy, "and you see my friends as rivals for my affection. So get over it already! I'm married to you, not them. Can't you see that? You're my husband, and they're just friends. It's not the same thing."

Michael is still wrapping his mind around the idea of jealousy.

"Maybe," he admits, thinking about it. "Maybe something like jealousy is what I'm dealing with. But the problem is still there. You still spend way too much time with them, and not enough time with me, and that's why we're sitting here in this office trying to work out our issues!"

Michael, jealous or not, has remembered his anger and frustration.

Amy, who was enjoying her role as teacher and mentor, is agitated by Michael's return to the core attack.

"Listen," she tells her husband, her voice rising in volume and her words coming at a quicker pace, "just listen to me. Nobody is going to tell me who I can see and who I can't see, or when I can go out with my girlfriends and when I can't go out with my girlfriends. If you think that just because I got married, I am now going to suddenly let somebody else tell me what to do, you're crazy."

Now, after a variety of false starts and partial explanations, we are getting to the core of the problem in the room. It's a problem of power and control over who is responsible for what. Who's the boss?

Who's the Boss? Biblically and Otherwise

In the comfort of a counselor's office in Oklahoma, Garrett and Cindy are discovering the origins of their current struggle. Each of them grew up in homes with very different styles of power and control and with highly dissimilar relationships between their parents. As they explore their family histories together, Cindy and Garrett realize that the problems they're facing in their marriage are entirely normal and, in fact, predictable, based on their families of origin.

"No wonder we're fighting about stuff like this," Cindy says at one point. "I'm amazed by how different our two families are. Why didn't we realize that earlier? Why didn't we talk about it when we got together? I mean, we talked about our families, but we never really looked at the way decisions were made or about simple things like who's the boss of the family," Cindy continues. "Now that we're learning all this, at least we know we're normal and these issues are normal."

Cindy relaxes into her chair, visibly less worried about the future of her relationship with her husband.

Meanwhile, Garrett has spent a great deal of time explaining how his father behaved as the leader of the home. He gestures as he talks, making eye contact with Cindy and also with the counselor.

Garrett is in an expansive, talkative mood.

"My dad," Garrett begins, "my dad, well, he'd be gone for days at a time, especially during hunting season. When us boys got older, he would take us with him, but before that he'd just be gone. I'm not sure about the longest time he was away, but I bet it was maybe two weeks or more," Garrett recalls.

"Never once did I hear my dad ask my mom's permission to go hunting or ask her if he could be away from the house for a week or ask her if she would be OK while he left us. He just went hunting! He was the man of the house, the husband of the marriage, the head of the family, and if he wanted to go out hunting, he went out hunting. That was that.

"He didn't have to fill out any forms or deal with any red tape," Garrett gushes. "There wasn't a review board looking over his shoulder. He just went hunting if he wanted to, when he wanted to. Life was simple because he was a man, and he was the boss of the house. He was the top of the food chain, and I guess I've always seen the husband that way," Garrett says. "I've just kind of assumed that one day, the top of the food chain would be me!"

Cindy is quiet, not arguing or countering her husband's explanations.

Without a fight on his hands, Garrett's energy sags.

"That's why I've been so uptight lately," Garrett realizes. "I've been angry because I grew up watching somebody else get to be at the top of the food chain, and then it finally got to be my turn, but then it was like the rules changed all of a sudden and everything was different.

"I like the rules I grew up with," Garrett says quietly, not arguing now. "I like the man being the boss of the house and the man being able to do whatever he wants to do. I grew up watching that happen, and knowing that someday, somehow, somewhere it would finally be my turn.

"Now," Garrett finishes his thought, "now it's like I really don't get a turn after all, and that's what makes me so angry."

* * *

Meanwhile Amy has a speech of her own.

"This isn't the 1950s," Amy is saying, mostly to the counselor. "This isn't some television sitcom from the fifties where the man is the head of the household and the woman is some domestic goddess, spending all her time in the kitchen."

Amy shakes her head.

"I thought we left all that behind us in the eighties," she fumes. "I mean, I thought someone getting married today was completely free from all those unwholesome stereotypes and all those ridiculous notions about a husband ruling over his wife, and a wife being mostly a cook, housekeeper, and mom to the kids."

Michael, greatly to his credit, has decided not to interrupt his wife.

Amy is not quite finished.

"I would never, ever, have gotten married in a society like that or a time like that," Amy continues. "If that was how married life was, I would have just stayed single all my life. I don't care what my parents would have said or anyone else would have thought. I would never give up my own personal freedom, just so some testosterone-loaded male could go on a power trip by bossing me around."

Amy glances around the office, making sure that she's been heard.

She has.

Michael looks across the table, wondering what the counselor will say or do now, and whether there is any way out of this dilemma.

After a pause, the counselor asks Amy about her family of origin. The discussion takes a variety of turns and raises interesting questions. Yet eventually, the core issue comes sharply into focus.

"My mom never really had a vote in how things were done," Amy recalls. "My dad was opinionated and bossy. Every night at the dinner table he'd be talking about politics or church or something else that had him upset. He was never a minister, but he preached around the dinner table almost every night."

Amy's tone changes as the thinks about her own mother.

"My mom had actually gone to college," Amy sighs. "Dad was a high school graduate who got drafted and went straight into the military. He came home from serving his country and got a job at the post office. He wasn't illiterate or stupid, but he didn't exactly read the classics or understand Shakespeare.

"My mom, on the other hand, was a lit major in college, and she wrote poetry, and she drew designs for clothing and even a few pieces of furniture. She was this artistic, well-educated, lively woman—and she ended up married to a guy who treated her like his personal servant.

"I used to look at my mother and wonder what she might have become if she hadn't gotten married, or at least if she hadn't married my dad. I mean, she had a ton of potential, and she's so smart, and she ended up stuck at home as a housewife with a husband who's not that smart, not that successful, and honestly, not even that nice to her."

Amy is suddenly aware that she's criticizing her father more than she originally intended. She backpedals somewhat.

"My dad is OK, he's just a typical guy from his era," Amy says quietly. "He's opinionated and outspoken, and he's not very well-read. So often, even when I was just a teenager, I could tell that he really didn't know what he was talking about. But that didn't keep him from talking!

"Meanwhile, across the table from him was this beautiful, articulate, well-educated woman who didn't even have a vote in where we lived, how we spent our money, or anything else. Dad ran the family, ran the household, and definitely won any and all arguments, if there were any. In our house the chain of command was very simple: Dad ruled and Mom served.

"Believe me," Amy explains near the end of her narrative, "I grew up being absolutely certain that I would never, ever, get stuck in a situation like that. I wasn't going to end up like my mom, no matter what."

Patterns and Our Programming

These two case studies, separated by geography and culture but happening at approximately the same time and to couples of approximately the same age, indicate how strongly our family histories can influence our understanding of power and control in the home.

Garrett, growing up in west Texas, was raised by a father who loved to hunt and fish and be outdoors. Garrett's father, as a lifestyle and as a practice, was not accountable to anyone about his whereabouts or his personal choices. As the man of the house, if he wanted to go hunting, he simply went hunting. There was no one to consult, no one's permission to seek.

Garrett interpreted the passivity of his mother as her implicit approval of this pattern. For Garrett, watching these two adults live out their marriage, being a husband meant being free to come and go, pick and choose, hunt and fish. Being a wife meant staying home and taking care of things while the husband was away. In Garrett's view, this isn't unfair or unjust. It's just how things are.

Meanwhile, Amy, who grew up in a different part of the country, also watched a household in which the male was dominant. To Amy, looking at matters from a rational point of view, one adult in her household was intelligent and educated, worldly and wise. The other adult in her home was much less so.

Surprisingly, the adult who lacked education got to be the boss while the wise and worldly adult was merely a passive companion. This, seen through the eyes of an inquisitive female child, seemed grossly unfair. From Amy's perspective, it made no sense that someone should rule the household, just because of his gender, when across the table was someone smarter and better informed about world events. Rather than accepting her mother's passivity, Amy was offended and angered by it, resolving to never be dominated by a male, to never surrender her intelligence or her education to someone with lesser or fewer gifts.

In both cases, it was helpful for the couples to unpack their personal and family histories in order to understand how their ideas and values had been shaped by the patterns that were lived out in front of them. Although we've explored only two of those family patterns here—Garrett's family, Amy's family—the other spouses also came from families with histories, patterns, and practices. So in each case, as a new couple was formed, there were two distinctly different points of view about how decisions should be made in a marriage or a family.

Courtship, a brief phase during which we show each other our best selves, presenting our identities in the best possible light, is rarely a time when serious and problematic family differences get discussed. If anything, the hormonal and relational buzz of courtship causes us to diminish problems and underestimate the extent of the difficulties that lie ahead as we establish a household.

This is why competent premarital counseling is so critically important. Somewhere in the midst of hormonal attraction and romantic enchantment, a qualified professional needs to help couples work through their family histories, with a special emphasis on issues of power and control in the home. There must be clear and extensive discussions of the ways our parents modeled their roles as father and mother, especially the ways in which they resolved disputes and made major decisions.

History tends to repeat itself.

Until we make intentional and often difficult choices, we are highly likely to repeat the patterns we witnessed as we grew up. Our spouses are likely to do the same. It's a recipe that is almost guaranteed to produce conflict. Like most conflict, it might have been avoided if we were better prepared in the first place.

Good counseling matters. Right from the start.

Power XPR Discussion Questions

1. Who was the most outspoken person among your parents or stepparents as you grew up? Was it a male or female? Did being outspoken and verbal translate into winning arguments in the home? When the adults in your home argued, who usually won? What did victory look like? How did the "defeated" partner handle his or her defeat after an argument?

2. Have you heard the term *servant leader* in church or in some other setting? Do you understand this term and concept? If so, would you describe the adult male in your home, if any, as a servant leader? Why or why not? To what extent were the males in your household as you were growing up rulers, leaders, or decision-makers? How did this shape your own understanding of male/female relationships?

3. How were major decisions such as where to live, whether or not to move, whether or not to accept a new job, and similar choices made in your childhood household? Did you get to witness the decision-making process? Did you

ever watch a significant disagreement between your parents over a major issue such as this? If so, how did the disagreement play out? Was the decision changed, deferred, or postponed if one person disagreed or had objections?

4. Describe a marriage that you've observed in which the husband is the clear and undisputed ruler in the home. In your view, is this marriage healthy and happy? Do both adults in the marriage seem completely satisfied with the balance of power in their relationship? If you could interfere with their relationship and change the balance of power, would you? Or would you prefer that each couple be given the freedom to work out issues of power and control within their own household and on their own terms?

5. What would you say to a young female if you believed she was marrying a man who was highly controlling? Would you discourage her from making the relationship a marriage union? Would you attempt to show the young woman that her potential future partner was domineering or bossy? How far would you go in trying to delay or prevent the marriage? Or would you prefer that each person be free to make a choice without outside interference?

6. Have you personally witnessed a marriage in which the woman seemed to control the family or the household? From your perspective, how did this seem to work? Did it seem normal and natural and acceptable? Did it make you uncomfortable on some level? Did you lose respect for the man in the relationship because, for your own reasons, you believed he was somehow less masculine if he allowed himself to be led or controlled by a woman?

7. If you believe in the idea of a fair and balanced marriage in which each person has an equal voice, have you ever witnessed a marriage like that up-close and observed how it worked? Do you base your idea of *fair and balanced* on a mentor couple in your church or your family circle? Approximately how many fair and balanced marriages have you seen in your life, and where have you seen them?

8. If you knew a young male who had grown up believing that the man is clearly the head of the household but that the man should "be nice about it, and not be a jerk," how would you discuss this concept with the young man? Would you argue with him or agree with him? To what extent is this young man's understanding similar to your own? To what extent is this young man's understanding incorrect and unhelpful, from your point of view?

9. Should being the boss flow directly from a person's gender, or should other qualifications be in play? Is the whole idea of being a boss irrelevant within a marriage, since no one should be the boss?

6
POWER

*Your Premarriage **Expectations***
About Power and Control

Vicki was single and gainfully employed for almost four years following college. By the time she married Brent, she had worked for a local banking company long enough to become a loan officer and assistant branch manager. With a business major and finance minor, Vicki's natural intelligence and her outgoing nature combined to help her move up the corporate ladder fairly quickly.

Marriage had always been a part of Vicki's hopes for the future, so she was happy to say yes when Brent proposed to her. They had been dating for about eight months; Vicki genuinely loved Brent and could see herself as his wife. Yet what surprised Vicki after her marriage was how very traditional Brent was in his understanding of gender roles within marriage.

"I loved him almost immediately," Vicki tells us today, "and I still do! He's just the greatest guy in the world. Everyone in my family loves him, and he's got a ton of friends. He's the kind of guy who will drop whatever he's doing to help you if you're in need. I don't know anybody who doesn't love and respect Brent, and that includes me. I think he's the greatest!"

Yet Vicki has sought marriage counseling, and Brent is with her, because the two are having frequent fights in the early months of their new marriage. The fights do not reflect a lack of love on either side. What the frequent fights indicate is that a struggle for power is already emerging in their marriage relationship. It's a struggle that is nearly universal and occurs in almost every marriage on the planet. The few exceptions are scary; they tend to involve people who are so unduly passive that they are likely to be taken advantage of or victimized by their partners.

This will not be happening to Vicki.

"I have a lot of responsibility at work," Vicki begins after the general introductions are done and everyone is settled into comfortable seats in the counselor's office. "I take my responsibility seriously. One reason I'm good at my job is that I don't make excuses, and I don't pass blame on to someone else. When I fail, I admit it. I don't try to hide in my office or deny reality. When I fail, I say so. When I succeed, I try to be generous and share the credit with others. When I succeed, I realize that I didn't achieve success on my own; a good team is also responsible.

"I also have a lot of authority in the bank," Vicki continues. "It's taken me a while to work my way up to positions of increasing authority, but right now I'm not only a senior loan officer, I am also an assistant branch manager. Our branch manager is out on maternity leave right now. So every day, I run our branch, and everyone knows it. Until the branch manager returns, mine is the final answer on any question that comes up. I am the top of the food chain at our branch office.

"Does this sound like I'm crazy for power and have to be in control?" Vicki asks out loud, looking around the office for some reaction as she speaks. "I'm really not like that—I don't think.

But here's the thing: All day long at work I have a lot of authority and control. Then I come home, and it seems as if I have no authority at all in anything!

"In the fifteen minutes of commuting time from work to home, I go from being a person who runs an entire branch office to a person with no voice and no vote in how we'll do things in our own marriage."

Brent interrupts for a moment to disagree with his wife.

"That's not true, honey," he insists. "I always ask your opinion about stuff."

Vicki looks intently at the counselor.

"Did you hear that?" she asks, referring to Brent's comment.

Reflective Listening

Across the ocean in a vastly different culture, a young married couple faces the same kind of problem but from a different perspective.

Abed and Miriam are not only new to marriage, they are also new to the concepts and theology of evangelical Christianity. Both of them were converted from a religious culture that has long been hostile to Christian thought, mostly due to historical and political reasons. Miriam and Abed came to belief in Christ at about the same time and are still largely formed by their culture of origin. Their marriage reflects more of their root culture than it does of New Testament thought.

Miriam and Abed's social system has long been strongly patriarchal, with women reduced to secondary roles that are subservient and docile. Women have no voice and no vote; they also frequently are denied their requests for education. Women can be beaten almost at will; the simplest of allegations will suffice. It is not unusual for a wife to face harsh and painful consequences if she goes against the slightest wish or instruction from her husband.

Abed grew up watching his father beat his mother; this process did and still does seem normal to him. "She deserved it, most of the time," is Abed's simple explanation of his mother's frequent experiences of being punished. "She was always speaking out very boldly, criticizing my father's choices. I watched him tolerate that for a while, then finally he would beat her. Sometimes he beat her very severely, but it always happened because she brought it on herself."

Miriam grew up watching her mother treat her father with utmost respect and deference. Miriam's mother was visibly and constantly afraid of being beaten. As a result of her fear, she remained passive and never voiced nor expressed any objection to whatever her husband wished, desired, or insisted upon. Miriam's mother was a model of passivity and acquiescence as a wife, meekly obeying whatever her husband instructed and directed.

Against this backdrop Miriam and Abed have embraced Christianity and were even married in a Christian wedding ceremony. But in the daily ins and outs of their new relationship, both tell us they are frequently confused.

"Mark and April, Christians who mentor us, keep telling us that a husband and wife are to be equal in marriage," Miriam says brightly. "And I want to believe them, because I see how strong their marriage is. But when I sit down to read the Bible, I read that wives should submit themselves to their husbands as unto the Lord."

Miriam smiles sweetly at a visiting counselor and his wife, seemingly without guile or hidden agenda.

"This teaching I understand," Miriam says with a shrug. "This is much the same as in my own family. What I do not understand is why Mark and April are telling us that a husband and wife are to be equal in marriage. Why do they tell us this, and what do they mean?"

Abed nods in agreement with his wife's question. Separately, he has issues of his own as he explores a belief system that he wants to embrace but does not yet fully comprehend.

"I am told to love my wife as Christ loved the church," Abed says with the earnestness of a young seminary student, "and this I wish to do fully. But what does this mean when it's time for us to make a decision about where to live or how much money to spend on something we want? Isn't Christ the ruler over the church? Doesn't Christ serve as the head of the church? So isn't Christ loving the church by leading it? Isn't He loving the church when He is firmly in control of what the church is going to do?"

Abed's question is neither cynical nor sarcastic; he is genuinely seeking to explore and understand biblical teachings about married life.

* * *

Both of these couples, separated by an ocean and their cultures, are struggling to understand how best to make decisions within their marriages. Should both parties in a marriage be given an equal voice, as Miriam and Abed are told? Or should one partner have the ultimate or final authority over a decision, as many people believe the Bible teaches about the husband and father's role in a home?

Within each home, this question is being played out in daily life. And it's the same in marriages around the world, especially in the first few weeks and months as a couple strives to find an identity together.

When two adults come together to form a marriage, each has an idea of how the new relationship will be conducted. A young woman, feeling very loved by the man who proposes to her, will often tend to assume that her position as a loved and cherished woman will result in her being respected, valued, and listened to. She is surprised to learn later that her husband desires her sexually and values her for her appearance, but he isn't ready to learn from her.

A young man, raised in a patriarchal household, may assume that everyone knows the basic rules of marriage and everyone follows them. He isn't violent or evil by nature, he's just accustomed to the man leading and controlling. So he assumes that when he gets married it's finally his turn to lead and control. He's the man, he has come of age, and he is now the head of a household. His day of authority is finally here. What a wonderful and welcome relief!

Rarely do two separate persons come to a marriage with exactly the same set of expectations, values, and desires. Generally speaking, each partner will have a somewhat different expectation of how issues like power and control will play out in the new relationship. In the artificial and contrived environment of courtship, it is impossible to locate any meaningful clues about future decisions. During the courtship phase of a relationship, which can include engagement and planning a wedding, both parties are acting abnormally and putting their best selves forward.

Later, as reality sets in, the difference in perspectives on power can be jarring and chaotic. Arguing and fighting, as we have observed already, is a normal and typical reaction to these control issues as they emerge. What matters is to disagree in a loving way, which is why enlisting the help of a counselor or minister can be so valuable. In the presence of a trained referee, we can fight fair and explain our differences to each other while also playing by the rules.

Referees are valuable; those who choose to charge for their services are worth their pay. They are earning their keep with every well-chosen word of instruction, correction, and guidance.

✳ ✳ ✳

Vicki and Brent love each other, yet Brent is not able to entertain the idea of a woman leading. "I love dancing," Brent says, "and I can even play the fiddle a little bit. I've been to barn dances to go dancing, and I've been to barn dances to play the fiddle while other people dance.

"When I'm out there dancing with a partner," Brent continues, "I'm going to be the one who does the leading! I think it looks utterly ridiculous when a man allows himself to be led around by a woman, even on the dance floor. I wouldn't respect a man like that, and I certainly wouldn't want to become one.

"I don't think men should be bullies or mean or unfair," Brent adds, "and I don't believe men are always right about everything. But I think dancing and marriage and family life and everything else works out a lot better when everyone knows who the leader is. And I think men are born to be the leaders!

"I'm not saying that to start a fight; I'm just telling you what I believe."

Vicki allows a moment of silence before adding her opinion.

"I understand everything you just said," Vicki tells her husband, looking directly at him, "but do you understand that I work in an office that is led by a woman? And right now that woman is me! When our branch manager does come back from maternity leave—if she does—she is a woman too.

"Every day of my life, I work in a system in which it doesn't matter whether you are a male or a female," Vicki continues. "What matters is what it says on the name plate on your desk.

"My name plate says Assistant Branch Manager. And that means I have a lot of authority and a lot of control in the bank. It also means I am held responsible when things go wrong, and I am accountable to a wide range of people for the financial results of our local branch. I've been given power because I've proven myself to be responsible, reliable, and capable."

Vicki makes a conscious effort to soften her voice and her tone.

"All I'm saying," Vicki says, again looking her husband directly in the eyes, "is that I'm ready to be responsible and capable at home too, not just in the office."

Brent has no immediate response to that.

✷ ✷ ✷

Miriam and Abed are thinking out loud.

"I do not believe that I should ever beat my wife," Abed says slowly. "When I try to imagine Christ beating His wife, this is impossible to imagine."

Miriam interjects to make an obvious point.

"The Christ was not married in this life," she explains.

"Yes," Abed agrees. "But can you take what you know about this man and imagine Him beating His wife because she spoke to

Him too sharply? Or because His food is not cooked to His satisfaction? Or beating her because His children are misbehaving?"

Miriam looks thoughtful.

"I am thinking about my mother," she says slowly. "My mother was afraid of my father at all times. I do not believe she would be afraid of the Christ. I believe she might love Him and respect Him, but I do not believe she would be afraid."

Miriam lowers her voice to almost a whisper. She looks around the room, which is occupied only by Miriam and Abed and two counselors.

"My mother has been afraid for as long as I have known her," Miriam sighs. "But as I think about the Christ, I do not believe my mother would fear Him."

"I believe you are right about this," Abed affirms to Miriam. "This is what I am thinking also. Perhaps we are making some progress together on this matter."

It's worth remembering—although it's not the topic of this book—that the Christian faith was birthed in the Middle East. It grew out of another Middle Eastern religious system known as Judaism. Christ himself was Jewish by birth and practice.

Somehow, when North American Christians seek to evangelize other cultures, they end up bringing much of North America with them. Christianity, which transcends cultures and races and eras, was not born in North America. It did not grow out of North American mind-sets or understandings. It is not rooted in popular North American ideas such as democracy or freedom. The roots of Christianity are much deeper historically; they spring from the birthplace of human culture itself—the Fertile Crescent.

As scholar Dean Flemming points out in his hugely helpful work, it is important to contextualize the New Testament—including its passages about marriage—in a way that translates genuinely and effectively into the life and practices of the host culture.

Brent and Vicki are working toward mutual agreement.

"I'm not trying to be the boss over you," Vicki assures her husband. "I have to be the boss of people all day long! I don't come home wishing for more people to boss around. In fact, I come home wishing more people would solve their own problems rather than complaining to me all the time!"

"That makes sense to me," Brent says, looking at his wife. "I have to tell you, I can't imagine myself being bossed around by a woman, certainly not in my own house. So it's really helpful to hear you say that you're not trying for that."

Vicki smiles. "I'm just trying to be recognized as a responsible adult with a lot of wisdom and a lot to offer to any situation," Vicki affirms. "I need you to see me that way. I need you to see me as a person who is smart and capable, someone whose opinion you would definitely value and respect."

"I can get there," Brent says with a sly look on his face. "It may take me twenty or thirty years, but I think I can get there."

Brent is kidding, and his wife knows it. So she kids him right back.

"I just need the light bulb to go on," she tells her husband. "Even if the switch takes a long time to operate."

These two are going to be OK.

Your Power XPT Discussion

1. As you think about being married in the future, how do you view the husband's role within a marriage? Do you see the husband as the leader of the home? If so, what does this mean in actual practice and in daily reality? Do you see the husband as having the final say on major decisions of married life? Do you see the husband as making the choices as the wife simply affirms these choices and goes along with them?

2. As you consider getting married and forming a new household, how do you view the wife's role within a marriage relationship? Do you see her as an equal partner who is on the same level as her husband in terms of decision-making and sharing the responsibilities? Or did you see her more like the vice president of the United States— important to be sure, but definitely second in command unless someone dies or goes out of office?

3. What does *equality in marriage* mean, and do you agree with this idea in any sense? As you think about being in a marriage, do you expect that each person in your marriage will have one vote and that both votes are equal? If so, how do you expect to break a tie when the two of you are not able to agree? Are all votes created equal, or does one partner have a kind of super vote that becomes the tiebreaker? What will you do when you just can't agree? How will you move forward?

4. Do you believe that either gender is naturally smarter, stronger, or more capable of leading than the other? If so, which gender do you view as stronger, smarter, or more capable? On what do you base your decision? Should

leadership in a relationship be a privilege that is reserved for the smarter or the stronger person? Why or why not? Do you believe the Bible teaches that a man is superior to a woman in any way or that a woman is of higher importance than a man in any way?

5. Regardless of your own gender and role, do you expect to have to ask permission from your spouse before you make a small or large purchase once you are married? Do you expect to be required to involve your spouse when it is time to spend money or choose where or how to live? Do you see each partner in marriage as being able to control his or her own private choices and decisions, or do you view marriage as a union that requires each partner to sign off on the major choices? If so, which choices are the major ones? How much personal autonomy should each partner have? How much control does each partner have over his or her own life and decisions? In what situations should that control apply, and be used?

6. Can you understand why Abed and Miriam take a gradual process and a thoughtful journey before arriving at the conclusion that Christ would not beat His wife? Do you realize that the question is speculative, since Christ never married? Have you ever tried to actively and sincerely think outside your own culture and look at key questions from another point of view and a different perspective? Talk about occasions when you have done so. What conclusions did you reach, if any?

7. How would you respond if two adults who consider themselves equals in their marriage are being criticized in their local church, because people in the church believe that a

man should always be the leader over the woman? Would you counsel them to change their understanding about marriage? Would you advise them to consider finding another church? Regardless of whether or not you agree with their perspective, how would you advise them to proceed when they are under attack from members of their own community of faith?

8. What percentage of the time do you expect you will be in agreement with your partner about major issues? Do you expect that the two of you will usually agree about major purchases, moving to another home or another city, how to discipline your children, and other such choices? Will you be surprised if the two of you end up having serious disagreements in these areas, or do you think serious disagreements happen only to others and won't happen to you?

Should an argument always be won by the person who makes the most rational, logical explanation of his or her choice? Or should an argument usually be won by the person who has the most authority or power in the situation, regardless of the logic of his or her viewpoint? Is logic what makes someone right about an issue, or does might make right in a discussion?

7
FAITH
*Your Premarriage **Experience** with Faith and Values*

Many couples get married despite being mismatched spiritually. Setting aside other variables—temperament, personality traits, personal likes and dislikes—it is surprising how many couples get together despite large differences in their views on religion, spirituality, faith, and values.

Many of these spiritual differences are easily visible while the relationship is forming, yet somehow the couples themselves seem oblivious. As with any other potential problem area, our involvement and participation in a romantic and affectionate relationship tends to cloud our view of reality. Women, especially, seem able to minimize spiritual differences. Even women who notice the differences while dating seem remarkably able to visualize themselves as helping, changing, or reforming their life partners after the ceremony concludes. These women appear to believe that their life partner, once he has a ring on his hand, will rapidly and sincerely grow an appetite for church attendance, men's Bible studies, and spiritual formation in general.

Long experience in marriage counseling indicates otherwise.

Adult Values Are Clearly Visible

Jennifer attended a Christian university for one year. During the following summer she and her parents mutually decided that the overall cost was no longer affordable. After considering her options, she attended a community college near her family home, graduated with an associate's degree, and quickly joined the workforce. By the time she began seriously dating she was a young adult with a good-paying job. Although she still lived at home, she had earned a degree, and her college transcript revealed a cumulative GPA of 3.4.

During her year at the Christian school, Jennifer went on a few dates but was not socially active, and no serious suitors emerged from that spiritual setting. Later, at the community college, Jennifer was a commuting student and was on campus only when she had classes to attend. Her social life, which was minimal, did not in any way grow out of the community college experience.

Jennifer eventually began to date a man she met at work. Previously married, he had been divorced for about two years and seemed to be a caring father to his young son, even though the ex-wife had primary custody of the child. In fact, watching her boyfriend care for his toddler-age son was one of the ways that Jennifer initially became attracted to and impressed with her coworker.

Very quickly, their relationship became serious. Although her parents never suspected, Jennifer became sexually active and, although she maintained the charade of living at home and was never absent overnight, she spent her free time at his apartment. Meanwhile, there was an increasing disconnect between Jennifer's long-held religious values and her lifestyle as a sexually active adult who was functionally living with a divorced partner.

As she began to consider marriage, however, Jennifer definitely wanted a church wedding. Even though she had feelings of guilt about her lifestyle choices, she considered herself a Christian. Even though her attendance at church had become quite irregular, she still considered herself an active churchgoer.

"I would never have married a guy who didn't share my values," Jennifer says now as she describes her dating and pre-engaged relationship. "Once we started getting serious I told Chuck that he and I needed to go to church together and that I definitely wanted a church wedding someday.

"Chuck was fine with that. I distinctly remember him telling me that he'd go to church with me, but not during football season. We both laughed at that. All I heard was that he would go to church. Looking back, what I should have heard was that his priorities were elsewhere—namely professional sports."

Jennifer eventually introduced her boyfriend to her parents. They had some concerns about his marital history, especially that he was already a parent. However, since he was clearly escorting their daughter to church and seemed to be receptive to spiritual truth, the parents decided not to make an issue of his personal history.

"I remember my mom telling me that maybe Chuck had grown up as a person through his earlier problems," Jennifer says now. "I thought that was a very wise perspective for my mom to have. Instead of criticizing my boyfriend, she was giving him credit for maybe maturing a bit, after some youthful mistakes."

Jennifer had been sexually active with her boyfriend and functionally living at his apartment for more than six months before she admitted the relationship and introduced Chuck to her parents. From that time until the wedding was another six months or so, and most of that time was spent planning a big ceremony, saving up for the expenses of married life, and arranging the details of a new life together.

"Will his son be in the wedding?" is a question Jennifer remembers her mother raising as the ceremony was being planned. Jennifer had already asked Chuck's son to be the ring bearer for them. Despite some initial flak from the boy's mother, Chuck's son was eventually green-lighted to be in the wedding, wearing a tiny tux and carrying the rings down the aisle to his father.

Her wedding day was the happiest day of Jennifer's life.

"All of a sudden I didn't feel guilty anymore," is how Jennifer remembers the early aftermath from the wedding. "Everything kind of came together. Now I wasn't this sinner who was having sex with a divorced man. I was a married woman, with a church wedding, and I had a ring on my finger. Brady (Chuck's son) was totally cute at the wedding, and my friends were actually jealous of me because I was becoming not only a wife but also a stepmom to a very cute little boy."

Jennifer's world seemed perfect, yet the spiritual mismatch between the newly married couple emerged rapidly and revealed itself to be serious.

True Colors

"Chuck just wouldn't go to church," is how Jennifer remembers those early days after getting married. "I begged him to go. I tried asking very nicely, and I tried offering him some kind of swap where I'd go do something with him if he would just get up on Sunday and come to church with me.

"He wouldn't do it. He had attended a few times when we were dating, enough that people knew him and liked him at church. He kind of had friends there, but it wasn't enough to motivate him to get there Sunday mornings. I wasn't even insisting that we go all the time, but I hoped we could be there a few times a month."

Jennifer was perplexed. She thought they had agreed that church attendance would be a regular occurrence in their marriage. Plus, on the weekends that they had custody of Brady, Jennifer wanted her stepson to be getting a high-quality Sunday School education, so he could grow up learning about God and giving his heart to God.

That wasn't happening. On the weekends when Brady was with them, neither Chuck nor his son went to church. Jennifer tried going by herself, but she considered it a disaster. Once she arrived in the parking lot, people began asking her where her husband was. Flustered by the question, she tended to lie. "He has a cold" or "He's not feeling well" or "He worked overtime yesterday" were her favorite responses, even though these things weren't true. Anything seemed better than admitting the truth: Jennifer had married a man who had no interest in spiritual things.

* * *

Cara's situation was entirely different.

"When we were dating, Sean made it very clear to me that he was an atheist and didn't believe in God," Cara explains to a counselor. "He was never sneaky about that; he never hid his beliefs. He told me over and over again that people could believe whatever they wanted; it was fine with him. He didn't see any harm if someone wanted to believe in God."

While this variance in perspective might not seem like a wise foundation on which to build a marriage, Cara was undeterred in her love for Sean. "We had so much in common," Cara says. "We liked the same music; we went to a lot of live plays and musicals. We were always doing things together. I really thought we were pretty much the same in how we looked at life and what our core beliefs were."

Cara missed the glaring exception to the couple's unity.

"He really changed after we got married," is how Cara interprets or reinterprets her own life history. "Sean started reading Sam Harris and some of the newer atheists. His attitudes began to change. He started getting angry whenever someone expressed a belief in God or talked about the importance of religion. Since my faith was important to me, it seemed like he was getting angry with me on a regular basis.

"For about two years, my husband made fun of me, was sarcastic about my faith and how simplistic it was, and basically called me an idiot for believing in God," Cara says quietly today. "For two people who had been drawn together by art and music, by ideas and reading, by a quest of discovery, I just really wasn't prepared to have my husband become so closed-minded and judgmental on this topic."

Cara shakes her head, still confused by the apparent change in her husband's tolerance for other values.

"I tried reading Sam Harris," Cara comments. "But I couldn't get past his anger. Plus, he really hadn't done his homework on the church fathers or on the origins of the Christian faith. He kept reacting against 'straw men,' and I didn't find his arguments compelling. Frankly, I think there are a lot more literate and interesting atheists out there. I don't see why Sam Harris is so popular."

After two years of ridicule and harassment by her husband, Cara admits that she sometimes thought of leaving him. But as a devout evangelical Christian, she didn't believe that option was open to her unless and until her husband was sexually unfaithful.

"As far as I know, we didn't have that issue," Cara explains. "To my knowledge, there wasn't anyone else. If there was, Sean did a great job of hiding it from me. I don't think he was involved with anyone."

Sean was the one who filed for divorce, catching his wife by surprise.

"He basically gave me an ultimatum," is how Cara remembers the situation. "He told me that unless I was ready to 'think like an adult' and have a wiser worldview and perspective, then he could no longer be married to me. He told me that he never intended to marry a child, and that he didn't plan to stay married to someone whose brain was switched off—someone who refused to do any real thinking."

Cara grows quiet in the moment.

"After two years of that, I was accustomed to his language," she sighs. "But the truth is, I was actively reading, growing deeper in my faith, and I was engaged in the same intellectual questions that interested us while we were dating. In fact, if anything, my husband's journey from atheism into extremism actually helped me. Thanks to Sean's constant badgering, I had to take my faith down to its roots and reexamine everything I believed.

"The process was hugely helpful for me," Cara says today. "And I came out the other side more grateful than ever for authors like Anne Lamott, Walter Wangerin, Frederick Buechner, and others. In those authors, just to name a few, I found a faith I could relate to, a faith that made sense in my daily life. Then when I would read more ostensibly religious writers such as Max Lucado or Rick Warren, my faith had a deeper underlying source to it."

Sean opted to divorce his wife, and Cara did not contest the process.

"Thank God we didn't have kids," Cara sighs. "We would have been fighting all the time about how to raise them, about what they ought to believe, about whether or not they could go to church, or which church. I can't believe I didn't think the differences in our spiritual values would matter in a marriage. Now I realize that my spiritual beliefs may be the ones that matter the most to me. Why didn't I see that before, when I was all starry-eyed and in love?"

Now divorced for several years, Cara is dating a graduate student who attends a seminary in the large city where she lives.

"We have amazing discussions," Cara smiles, her face lighting up as she speaks. "I don't know whether this relationship is going anywhere, but for right now, it's a deep friendship, and we have heart-to-heart discussions about absolutely everything, including how kids ought to be raised.

"I'm hesitant to use the phrase, but I guess this is a counselor's office, so I'll just be blunt," Cara continues. "After having such a bad experience in my first marriage, right now I sometimes feel as if I've found my soul mate!"

Cara interprets the counselor's nod as agreement.

"I'm not rushing into this," she explains to the counselor. "I'm really not. But I can't tell you how absolutely refreshing it is to find someone who shares my same faith and who even loves the same authors. We went to hear Anne Lamott speak at a conference a few months ago, and we both loved it! Even though I think our faith is more fully developed than hers, we both like how honest she is, how brutally candid she is with her questions and her personal journey.

"That's the kind of faith I want," Cara insists, "a real faith in which I strive to please God and keep trying, even when I fall short. I want my kids to know that I'm human, that I'm not always perfect, but that God loves me anyway.

"To me, that's the heart of the Gospel message."

Faith and Values

From among a wide number of possible case studies, we've chosen these two because they so clearly illustrate the importance of choosing a life partner who shares your faith and values. Differences that seem minor at the start are magnified by the passage of time and the ongoing process of maturing into adulthood. What begins as tolerance early in the relationship can harden into a critical and judgmental attitude toward those who believe in a different way. Just ask Jennifer.

Although anyone can change his or her views along the journey of life, and although many come to a genuine faith as adults, our foundation of faith is often laid for us during childhood. For those who grow up in the church, faith begins in religious training such as Sunday School, then continues with defining experiences such as youth camps and retreats or college chapel services.

By the time a churchgoing child reaches adulthood, he or she has been spiritually formed by a wide range of teaching times, adult mentors, and personal experiences of faith in action. This faith may be especially developed and impacted if a teen or young adult has participated in a mission trip; worked at a homeless shelter or another social services setting; or in some way acted out the precepts of faith by doing community development, church planting, or feeding the hungry.

An adult who has been shaped by these values and beliefs would be wise to take a careful look at the values, beliefs, and spiritual ideas of any person he or she might date, become serious about, or consider marrying. At the very least, even if there was a general form of agreement about Christianity or Christian principles, there is a good prospect that the two adults might have varying levels of commitment to their faith and thus very different perspectives about how their faith would be lived out in the context of marriage and raising a family. Faith matters.

When we ignore our own faith formation and that of our potential life partner, we do so at our own peril. Somewhere in the future, after the hormonal rush is ebbing and the daily reality of marriage has set in, the differences in core values and spiritual perspectives may be larger than we realized.

Faith XPR Discussion Questions

1. Describe the faith and values of your parent or parents. In what ways did you observe your father and mother live out their spiritual beliefs? Did they primarily express their beliefs by attending church, or were there deeper issues such as tithing, serving as leaders of ministries, helping with child care, and other ways that your parents were

involved in their community of faith? Did you grow up watching a faith that was mostly lip service—talked about but not lived? Or did you grow up watching faith in action as your parent or parents actively made choices based on their spiritual values?

2. Talk about your own faith development as a child. Did you have an experience of coming to faith while you were growing up, during your student years from toddler to sixth or seventh grade? Evangelists such as Billy Graham often invite people to walk to an altar, kneel and pray, and there receive Christ as personal Savior. Did you have an experience like this during your childhood? If so, can you remember the context and setting? Were you in church, at a children's camp, or revival services? How old were you, and to what extent did you understand what you were doing and pledging? Was the experience real to you as a child? Did it affect your ongoing life and behavior?

3. Thinking about your teen years, roughly from mid-high school through college age, did you fall away from faith, or were these years formative to your faith? Did you have an experience of accepting Christ during your teen years, perhaps at a youth camp or during a mission trip? Talk about one of the most dramatic spiritual events of your own teen years. Process what that event meant to you and whether or not it changed your behavior. Did you have a mentor, leader, or someone else whose faith you admired and who helped shape the faith you hold today? If so, talk about that person and how he or she impacted your life. You may wish to send an e-mail or text message to that person if you are still in contact with him or her today.

4. Have you heard the term *social gospel*? If so, what does it mean to you? As you were growing up, did you experience situations in which believers came together to do good works in the community or perhaps to do missions service overseas? Did you participate in projects such as this? If so, how did these projects affect your own personal faith development and religious thinking? If Jesus was physically alive today, to what extent do you believe He would be actively engaged in helping the poor, caring for the ill and the elderly, and serving "the least of these" in our global society?

5. To what extent, if any, was a local church involved in your own personal spiritual formation? Did your spiritual experiences tend to happen in church or prompted by church services and events? Did the church provide adult mentors and spiritual leaders whose examples you wanted to emulate and follow? Were church services meaningful? Were sermons a chance to learn about spiritual matters, or did you mostly tune out during sermons? Talk about your experiences, both positive and negative, with church attendance and with involvement in a local church setting.

6. What size church or churches have you been actively involved in as a child, teen, or adult? In your opinion, what size church is best? What are the values and advantages of being involved in a smaller church—one that is less than one hundred in regular attendance and participation? What are the advantages of a church that has two hundred or three hundred persons attending? What can larger churches offer that is lacking in smaller congregations? What do bigger churches sacrifice that smaller con-

gregations enjoy as a regular feature of church life? What about very large churches—megachurches—that sometimes have thousands of people in their congregations? In your view, are such churches good places for faith development? Are bigger churches better than small churches at preaching, teaching, or other aspects of the life of faith? Or do you actually prefer a smaller church as a place to connect, learn, and grow? Why or why not?

7. While you were growing up, did you ever consider becoming a youth leader or a youth pastor? Did you ever feel called by God to do missionary service overseas, go into the ministry, or to study biblical or religious courses? If you experienced any of these, how have you followed up on these ideas as an adult? Is your adult life impacted in any way by your earlier desires or callings to serve God in a direct, frontline way?

8. Do you know married couples you would describe as "unequally yoked" in their spiritual values? What do you see as the unique challenges these couples face? What are the struggles that you see in these couples as they adapt to life together, especially as they raise their children? Of these unequally yoked couples you know, how many do you believe would be thriving in healthy marriage despite core differences in religious values and beliefs? In your opinion, can two people be soul mates if they disagree on central spiritual ideas and practices? Why or why not?

8
FAITH

*Your Premarriage **Expectations***
About Faith and Values

Len seemed to have very little interest in church and religion—until the church his wife attended began talking about putting together a trip to Ecuador. Unknown to anyone else, including his wife, Leonard had always dreamed about traveling to Central and South America. He had grown up reading about silver mines, coffee fields, and daring escapes through the jungle. In Len's imagination, both Central and South America were places of endless adventure.

Leonard had grown up dreaming about these places, and suddenly Sarah was coming home from church talking about Ecuador! In spite of himself, Leonard was interested right away. A small group of people—twenty or twenty-five at the most—would spend up to three weeks in in a remote village in Ecuador, doing construction projects and helping the local people.

Len was immediately intrigued. He began attending meetings at which the project was explained. The more he learned, the more this opportunity seemed like a once-in-a-lifetime chance to actually visit the mountains and jungles of South America. He had long dreamed about these places: Now he could actually go there and see them!

The cost of the trip was not unreasonable. "After all, we're going over there to help people," Leonard told himself and others. "It's kind of normal to expect us to bear the burdens of that expense. We're doing this to help out someone else!"

Sarah was amazed at this sudden transformation in her husband.

"I was able to drag him to church from time to time, but I could never get him to attend anything except Sunday morning worship," Sarah remembers. "I'd get him there maybe once a month, except during football season when he wouldn't go for any reason. I could never get him interested in a men's Bible study or a guys' night out or a weekend spiritual retreat.

"All of a sudden," Sarah says with a wide smile, "my spiritually apathetic husband was going to meetings at church, arriving early and staying late, talking to people about what kinds of construction skills would be needed and what kinds of projects the group would be working on. I couldn't believe it!"

Due to the overall costs of the trip, Sarah initially believed that perhaps Leonard would be the only one of them who could go. "I was fine with that," she claims. "I had never seen Len so worked up and excited about a church event. If I had to stay home while he went down there to help, that was OK with me, even though I was the one who first found out about the trip and first got interested in it."

It was Leonard who figured out a way to put the cost of both of them going into the family budget, because Leonard wanted his wife to come along also. It was Leonard who eventually decided to sell his prized bass boat, donating the money to a fund to help a local church in Ecuador reach its community for the cause of Christ.

"Over and above the costs of the trip, we were raising money for the materials we would need, and we were hoping to give some money to the local church there," Sarah recalls. "We were newly married and we were both working, but it's not like we had extra cash. I was completely stunned when Len advertised his boat online, sold it on a Saturday, and put the money toward our trip and also toward the church donation.

"I kept thinking to myself: is this the same man I married? What has happened to him all of a sudden?"

Fast forward to today. Leonard and Sarah have participated in three mission trips together, and they are busy planning their fourth.

"This is in our bloodstream now," Leonard grins. "Our kids are going to grow up watching Mommy and Daddy travel overseas every year or two to help other people. What do you think our kids will learn from that? What kind of values are they going to grow up with?"

Leonard is just getting warmed up.

"I can't wait until I have a son who is old enough to work right along with me," he exclaims. "Or if I have a daughter first, she better be enough of a tomboy to know how to use a hammer. She better be strong enough to push a wheelbarrow full of mortar."

Sarah smiles across the table at her husband.

"I'm just so proud of him!" Sarah tells us. "He's really taken the lead on this, and now it's a natural part of our marriage and our family."

Sarah rubs her stomach, not yet visibly expanded to give any evidence of what she's about to tell us.

"We're expecting our first," she smiles. "We haven't decided yet if we want to know our baby's gender. But we have decided that we want our baby to grow up watching his or her parents serve other people on mission trips."

"Amen to that," says Leonard, grasping his wife's hand.

Later in the same week we meet with Adele in a crowded coffee shop near her home in Queen Creek, Arizona. Adele has attended a conference at which we shared our seminar "Becoming Your Husband's Best Friend." We have a book by the same name, which contains much of the material from the seminar.

Greeting us after one of the sessions, Adele has asked us if we have time for a counseling appointment during our visit to the Phoenix metro area. We tell her we'll pray about it—and we do so. By prayer we realize that Adele is a divine appointment for us, so we agree on a time and place to counsel with her.

Meeting Adele for the first time, we quickly get a sense of her daily reality at home. Like so many women we meet across the United States and literally around the world, Adele is a partner in what we term a spiritual mismatch—in other words, Adele and her husband hold very different perspectives and views about matters of faith and values, spirituality and religion.

"He might as well be an atheist," Adele tells us as we sip coffee that is still too hot to drink. "He says he believes in God, but he also says that he doesn't believe in the church. He thinks church is a fraud. He thinks most preachers are frauds who just want to grab other people's money and put it into their own pockets. Every time there's a new scandal or a new headline, my husband tells me about it. Every time some preacher does something stupid, my husband makes sure that I know about it."

Adele wrinkles her face into a frown.

"The irony of it is, the one time I actually got him to come to my church with me, he ended up liking the preacher! He and the preacher kind of connected with each other, and I noticed that my husband paid attention during the sermon. I wasn't expecting that. But he's made no effort to go back, and when I invite him I get the same old speeches about phonies and frauds, money and scandals."

* * *

Adele sighs loudly, then takes a sip of her coffee.

"When we were dating, I thought both of us had the same beliefs about God and religion," Adele tells us. "He had a Bible in his home, and he would sometimes refer to a Bible verse when we talked about things. He was OK with us having a church wedding, and when we were meeting with the minister and preparing to get married, I never heard any speeches about frauds and scandals."

She is pensive for a moment. "When I think it through carefully, I realize that we never really discussed spiritual matters in depth," she admits. "I was kind of assuming that he cared about the same things and believed the same things. I do remember us talking about having kids. I said I wanted our kids to grow up going to church, and he didn't argue with me about that. I assumed we were on the same page."

It's an assumption made by far too many women as they contemplate marriage to men whose true spiritual values may be far different from their own.

* * *

Sarah saw it coming, but minimized it. "I guess I thought I could win him over," is how she rationalizes her choice to marry Leonard, even though she realized their perspectives were very different. "Leonard told me while we were dating that he was completely OK with me going to church on a regular basis, but he hoped I would respect his choice to just go occasionally. Len said he wasn't opposed to church in general; he just didn't see why anyone needed to be there Sunday after Sunday in addition to other times during the week for meetings, small groups, and other events.

"I know too many church people who are kind of crazy," is how Sarah remembers Leonard expressing it. "I believe in God just like they do, but I don't have to become a crazy person about it. I think it's important that I stay normal and believe in God in my own way. I don't want my kids or my neighbors or my friends or my family to think I'm one of those crazy people."

Reminded of his past statements, Leonard does not deny making them. "Some of those crazy people are among my best friends now," he laughs. "One of them, this guy at church who is in his seventies, is maybe my best friend in the whole world now. We've worked together on two projects, side by side, and I've gotten to know him kind of heart to heart. We've talked about absolutely everything while we were up on ladders, crawling around on a roof, or mixing mortar.

"Ralph is one of those crazy people I always talked about, so serious about God and so sold out for his church, but I have to tell you he is also a real person. He's a lot like me, just a way-older version of me.

"I guess," Leonard admits with a slight grin on his face, "I guess if I was honest I'm probably turning into one of those same crazy people more than I'd like to admit. Honestly, going on these trips has totally changed my views about God and church and religion. I get it now: Faith matters. And we don't grow in our faith by staying home and watching television. We grow by getting together with people and getting into God's Word."

Sarah sits wide-eyed in wonder. "Listen to him," she tells us with evident joy. "Just listen to him!"

✳ ✳ ✳

We ask Adele about her premarital counseling.

"Well, we didn't have much of that," Adele admits. "We met with the pastor a time or two, but that was mostly to plan the wedding. What I remember is that the pastor kept telling us that marriage was a holy obligation and a holy relationship—and a holy sacrament or something like that.

"I kind of tuned him out," Adele shrugs. "He wasn't talking about how difficult it might be to get along or how different we might turn out to be later. He was talking about spiritual things, and he was way over my head most of the time."

"And if he was way over my head," she continues, "I'm guessing that Jim probably tuned him out also.

"We met with the pastor two or three times. We filled out this work sheet about the order of service and who would be in the ceremony, and the pastor talked to us about holy this and holy that.

"I'm sorry," Adele confesses, "but that's about all I can remember from our premarital counseling. None of it had to do with real life or real issues."

✳ ✳ ✳

The secular world is full of wives like Adele and husbands like Jim. The religious world of faithful church attenders whose core values matter deeply to them is full of couples like Sarah and Leonard in their "before" experience prior to all of the mission trips.

Couples come together in a rush of hormones and a buzz of emotions. Women who are spiritually mature tend to lose their perspective, glossing over any differences they sense or realize in their prospective husbands. Men put their best foot forward, going along with church attendance or a church wedding in order to make peace and get the ceremony done.

Simply having a church wedding does not make you a spiritual couple or a faith-filled family. Going through the motions of a religious ceremony does not mean your home will be dedicated to God or that your family will model and live out the daily life of holiness.

Real faith takes practice—daily practice, weekly practice, practice that is lived out in a community of believers. Real faith is not about the brand name of your church or the identity of your denomination. It is about seeking God with a whole heart, desiring Him, and placing Him first in your life.

Far too many wives understand these things and hope their relationships will move in these directions. Far too many husbands live out spiritual apathy as their daily reality, either unbelieving at heart or indifferent to the demands of faith.

We call these relationships spiritual mismatches. To be sure, there are cases and situations where it is the husband who is on fire for God while the wife is less interested or less involved. Such cases occur and exist. Yet expressed as a percentage, the vast majority of spiritual mismatches reflect a committed wife who is married to an unspiritual or apathetic husband.

Much future conflict can be avoided by sharing your expectations with each other before marriage. Much future conflict can be avoided by resisting the temptation to assume that you understand your partner's perspective and the depths of his or her religious values.

Listed below are topics for discussion that will help you move toward a better understanding of your own values and your partner's values so that you can avoid becoming a spiritual mismatch after your marriage.

As stated earlier, when we ignore our own faith formation and that of our potential life partner, we do so at our own peril.

Out there in the future, after the hormonal rush is ebbing and after the daily reality of married life has set in, the differences in our core values and spiritual perspectives may be larger than we realized. The time to uncover our differences and explore our expectations is right now—before we say "I do."

Your Faith XPT Discussion

1. How often do you expect to be attending services at a local church as a married couple? Does your church offer more than one weekend worship service? Does your church offer midweek programming? Does your church have adult small groups that meet weekly in addition to a full range of activities and events for children and youth? How involved in these daily and weekly events do you expect to be? Why?

2. Will you be attending the same church that one of you grew up in or has been attending regularly as a single

person? If so, is the new partner fully in agreement about attending that church? Does the new partner feel as welcome, included, and comfortable in the services and social events at that church as the person who is already attending? What would you do if shortly after you were married the new partner expressed some discomfort with this particular local church? How would you resolve this issue?

3. In your own experience, what are the primary benefits of attending church? What are the main reasons a couple or family might want to make regular church attendance a part of their lifestyle? Are all of the benefits of maintaining a healthy spiritual life about going to heaven, or are there present-day, real-world benefits right here and right now? Talk about these benefits, if any.

4. As you raise your own children, if any, will you expect them to attend church with you? Will they be required to attend, and if so, will there be an age or a time when you will let them make their own decisions about going to church? How would you respond if you raised a child in church, yet as that child became a teen or an adult he or she wanted to quit attending? At what point would you allow your child to make his or her own decision about matters of faith and values, religion and spirituality, and church involvement?

5. Who will be the spiritual leader in your home? Which of you will take the lead in establishing family patterns and explaining family values with regard to church participation, personal spiritual life, and any family practices that reinforce spiritual values? Do you believe the male

should always be the leader in such areas and ways? Or do you believe that one of you who is already more spiritually tuned-in should probably take the lead?

6. How often do you pray together as a couple, even now if you are not yet married? When you do pray together, does each of you pray aloud so that the partner can hear you praying? If you have not yet tried this practice, would you be open to it or afraid of it? Does it seem too personal to pray aloud while in the presence of another person, even your life partner? Are you shy about these things or reluctant to pray aloud? Do you expect to always hold the same opinion about these matters that you hold today?

7. Do you expect to have some kind of daily devotions together as a couple after you are married? If so, have you already begun that practice? Are you having any kind of regular devotional time with your potential life partner? If you plan to have devotions as a couple, how do you see this working itself out in daily life? Is this likely to be a morning practice or an evening one? Are you likely to read from the Bible, read a good book together, or use a daily devotional guide such as those published by many churches and groups? If you plan to have devotions as a couple, will you take turns being the leader and reader in this practice, or do you expect one partner to always be the reader and leader? If so, which partner?

8. As you have children, would you expect to involve them in a daily family devotional time? What might this time look like or sound like? Do you picture your family all praying aloud while together so that each person hears

the others praying? Do you picture your family studying Bible stories together or studying the Bible itself together? What kind of spiritual experiences do you want your children to have within their own home and within their own family circle—not counting the spiritual experiences they may have at church, in Vacation Bible School, away at a summer camp, and so forth?

9. In general, do you prefer smaller churches or larger ones? What are the benefits of attending a large church? What are the drawbacks that come with increased attendance and increased crowd size in a larger congregation? What are the benefits and blessings of a smaller church? Why might someone choose to be involved in a small church, even if larger churches were nearby in their local community? Why is involvement in a small church a positive or beneficial thing for one's spiritual growth? What are the drawbacks that come with attending a smaller community of faith?

10. If your own church was sponsoring a mission trip, would you have an interest in being included? Why or why not? If you had interest, would you be willing to make personal and financial sacrifices, giving up vacation time and hard-earned money in order to go somewhere and work hard on behalf of others? How does a spiritual practice such as going on a mission trip benefit a couple or family? Beyond the benefits to a local church overseas, what are the potential benefits to those who serve on the team, support the team, and travel away from home in order to help someone they have never met? What are

the potential benefits to children who watch their parents behave this way?

11. When you hear of a television preacher or someone else who is caught in a major mistake or sin, does this convince you that all preachers or spiritual leaders are fraudulent and phony? Or does this remind you of the need to pray for and support your own pastor and spiritual leaders, all of whom are human and in need of prayer, support, and encouragement? When people fall or fail, does this mean God doesn't exist, or does this mean that even someone in a highly visible position of leadership is not exempt from the exact same temptations, struggles, and problems that beset us all?

9
FAMILY

*Your Premarriage **Experience** with Family Life*

When we join our lives together with another, we are joining more than simply a lone individual person. We are also joining that person's family circle and becoming a part of that person's complex network of family relationships and family experiences. In a world of brokenness, transition, and change, we may be joining a more complicated reality than we bargained for.

Accordingly, it's useful to study our family histories, not just in terms of major issues like money, sex, and power, but also in terms of how our families imagined and lived out family life. We may discover that our potential partner comes into a new relationship with a vastly different understanding of family values.

Simply put, how were our families fashioned and how did they function? How did our families of origin understand and live out what it means to be family? What did they demand, expect, or require from each member of the family? To what extent were those demands and expectations reasonable and realistic?

It's a conversation couples embarking on marriage need to have.

Eight years ago, Bryce was a promising young seminarian at a prominent school in western Canada. After a couple of internships at growing churches, he was already visible and on the radar of several large-church pastors and at least one district superintendent in the area. Bryce was warm, personable, intelligent, and a gifted communicator in the pulpit.

Beyond these tangible gifts Bryce also possessed an intangible quality of leadership that drew others to him. Although we can't always define or quantify this leadership trait, we know it when we see it; and Bryce had it. It's the quarterback in the huddle who goes on to win the college or professional football game. It's the talented account executive who leads the sales team, then becomes vice president of sales or marketing. It's the entry-level employee who moves into the corner office as CEO of the entire company.

Great leaders draw others to them. They are charismatic in a personal—not theological—sense. They work from an inner confidence that is winsome to others. Often this confidence derives from physical attractiveness, skills and abilities, or a high level of achievement.

Bryce was on the road to a plum ministry assignment, right from the start. His gifts and graces for ministry were numerous and evident. His personality was outgoing and positive, and he was inclusive of others by nature. He had a sunny disposition and many friends.

Midway through seminary, Bryce began to date a friendly young woman who attended a large church near the campus. Although always popular, Bryce had not been in many serious dating relationships. Friendly to a fault, he lost his heart rather quickly and became intensely focused on this specific young woman as his future mate. He began talking and thinking about marrying her.

Several seminary professors and a few close friends raised red flags.

"Martina is a great person," one of them told Bryce, "but is she going in the same direction with her life that you are going with yours? Does she share the same goals and the same sense of God's calling that you have? Regardless of your feelings about her personally, can you imagine her being your partner in leading a church family? Can you see her as a role model for other women and as a potential leader for women's ministries?"

Some of these questions were obviously unfair; the questioner simply hoped to get Bryce to see the lady he was dating from a more objective point of view. Bryce, for whatever reasons, was unable to do so. As a warm, compassionate, caring person he was fully invested in this specific relationship to the exclusion of all other potential romantic interests. For Bryce, the matter had been settled very early in the dating relationship as the couple got better acquainted. Bryce's interest in women quickly narrowed to an interest in just one woman: Martina.

"It's almost as if they're married already," one professor lamented as he watched Bryce get involved with a woman the professor termed "the wrong person for him, although I do like her otherwise. She's a fine human being; she's just not a good fit for Bryce. And she's a terrible fit for his future."

During his final year of seminary Bryce proposed to the young woman, and she quickly accepted. The two made plans to marry as soon as Bryce graduated. Although Bryce himself was happy, those who knew him best were disappointed that he was choosing "a wonderful person who simply didn't fit the profile of the ministry and leadership for which Bryce seemed destined."

Fast forward to today. Bryce and his wife live in the Pacific Northwest; they are the parents of two children with a third on the way. Bryce, who was a solid A student in both Hebrew and Hermeneutics, works at a large home improvement store in a busy suburban location. Still cheerful as always, and obviously gifted as a leader, Bryce is one of several assistant managers of the store and is frequently offered further training and substantial promotions. Yet, because these promotions would involve traveling to other locations and at least temporarily working in and managing other stores, Bryce always declines. By all available indicators Bryce will be an assistant manager at the same branch store well into the foreseeable future.

The reason? Bryce, husband and father, is voluntarily restricted to living within a fifty- or sixty-mile radius of his wife's hometown. It's a nonnegotiable condition his future bride established as they were planning to get married. For Martina, it was the most important aspect of their prospective marriage relationship. No matter what Bryce did for a living or pursued as a career, the new couple would need to live within an hour's driving distance of Martina's parents and her family circle. Nothing outside that radius could be considered.

Not yet married but already totally in love, Bryce minimized this requirement and didn't seem to think it presented an obstacle for him. He told himself that he'd simply find a church near Martina's family home, submit his résumé to that church, and then get to work. Yet even for a bright and promising seminarian, life did not exactly align with this simplistic perspective. There were few churches of his own denomination in the immediate area, and the few that existed tended to be smaller and unable to afford a full-time senior pastor. They were not interested in hiring staff and didn't have the budget to do so, even though several of the pastors told Bryce he was gifted for ministry and they'd love to have him on board.

Six months after getting married, one of the seminary's most promising young students was giving up on getting a ministry assignment within the tiny circle of geography that was permissible for him. Instead, he began applying for jobs at department stores, markets, and even a restaurant. He was delighted when the home improvement store hired him at a low hourly rate. He went to work immediately.

Today, Bryce's wages are enough to feed his family. Bryce's studies in theology, leadership, congregational life, and ministry are not being used in his daily employment. His closest connection to direct ministry comes on Wednesday nights when he plays drums for a youth service at church. However, his wife has already served notice that, as their third child is born, she will need Bryce at home on Wednesday nights instead of away at work or church.

Bryce, believing in the sanctity and permanence of the marriage bond, has chosen his partner for life. On a daily basis he is living with the consequences of his choice. He appears to be happy, and he speaks only positively about Martina. All who know Bryce wish him well, although some of them express sorrow that Bryce is not moving forward toward his calling in ministry.

"It's his life to live," says a denominational leader in a candid moment of observation and analysis. "But the greater loss is to the church at large. Bryce is gifted for ministry in ways that most young men are not. By now, several years after his seminary experience, he would be leading a growing church as the senior pastor, or perhaps he would have planted a church somewhere.

Any church he planted would be growing and thriving today. Of that I am very certain."

The man shakes his head slowly. "There is absolutely nothing wrong with selling lumber," he says distinctly, "and that's not what I'm saying. What I'm saying is this: Bryce's job is a waste of a talented and gifted young lead pastor or staff member. I ache for the loss of his ministry."

Family Matters

As we come together to form a new union, discussing our family histories is one of the most important conversations we can have together. And we don't mean one conversation; we mean a series of conversations that explore how our families of origin lived out family relationships and expressed the nature of being a family in their common life together.

Understanding these things about our own histories is absolutely crucial to helping us plan a future. Unless we understand these core issues, we will not be prepared for the contours and challenges of the road ahead. We will be surprised by the way our histories intrude into the present and shape the future.

Whether we draw charts and graphs about our family backgrounds, fill out complicated questionnaires about family histories, or simply converse about these issues, the reality is that the nature and character of our family histories will have a huge impact on the nature and character of our life together as a married couple.

This will be true in the major areas we've already discussed, like money, sex, and power. Yet the impact of our families of origin will include even the smaller categories and the unexpected margins of our new relationship. We'll discover surprises at holidays and on major occasions, yet also in our daily lives.

When you marry, you are not just marrying one person. You are literally marrying that person's family of origin and that person's experiences with the way a family lives out its life together. So by all means, explore the contours of each of your family's relational styles and behavioral patterns. It is a conversation worth having, and you should have it before saying "I do."

✳ ✳ ✳

For Megan and Jamie, the situation was just the reverse of Bryce and Martina. In their case it wasn't the wife's family that wanted a tight circle of geographically close connections; it was the husband's mother who could not or would not let go of her stronghold over her son.

"While we were dating, I really admired Jamie's relationship with his mom," Megan tells us during a difficult, intense session of counseling with the couple. "Ironically, it was that relationship that impressed me about Jamie. I watched my future husband be sacrificial, generous, and compassionate toward his mother, and that really endeared him to me. Jamie was a gentleman and a wonderful, caring son. I remember thinking that any mother would be blessed to have a son like Jamie!"

Yet even in the first few months of marriage, the problem signs were as clear as the proverbial handwriting on the wall.

"His mom would call us at all hours," Megan remembers. "It seemed that she would especially call in the evenings, just about the time we were ready to settle down and snuggle together as a couple. We'd finish a great meal together, maybe put on a DVD, and before you know it—ring! There would be his mom on the phone.

"She'd have some reason why she needed Jamie to drop everything and come over and help her out. She was always apologetic, but the apologies didn't seem sincere. She'd be all like, 'I'm so sorry to bother you about this, it's such a small thing,' but the following night she'd have another small thing. And the next night, it would be another small thing. It was always a small thing, and she was always 'sorry' for it. But she kept right on calling us anyway. If you really felt sorry for doing something, wouldn't you quit doing it? Wouldn't you change your pattern?"

Jamie interjects to defend his mother.

"My mother's a widow," Jamie tells the counselor. "My dad died a few years ago and Mom really doesn't have anyone to do even the simplest chores around the house. My sister lives nearby, but her husband doesn't get very involved with our side of the family. He's been distant and aloof from the moment he married Janet. So if any guy is going to do any project around my mom's house, I'm the only help she has. I'm the only person she can rely on when she needs something. Like it or not, it comes down to me."

"But it always comes down to you," Megan interjects. "And it always seems to come down to you right in the middle of an otherwise great evening, just as the two of us might get romantic or cuddly—or more than that."

Jamie shakes his head.

"I'm sure that's not Mom's intention," he says.

Megan's response is ready and rehearsed. "Maybe not, but whether or not it's intentional, the only thing wrong with our love life is that your mother keeps preventing it!"

Several sessions later the couple is describing their original intention to live in a different city three states away along the coast. This possibility was well in view as the couple was preparing for marriage and planning their new life together. Both of them are in agreement on how much they wanted to move away, walking through a door that God seemed to be opening just for them.

Jamie had interviewed for a significant job with a Fortune 500 company. The interview went well, and Jamie was invited back for a second interview. Two interviews and three lengthy phone calls happened; then Jamie was formally offered a high-paying job about a thousand miles away from his mother.

"I was ready to take that position," Jamie tells us in the counseling session. "They were offering me more money than I'd ever expected to make in my life. Beyond the money they were offering me a chance to move up the corporate ladder. I could see myself succeeding there, doing what I was trained to do.

"We were talking about me moving out there before the wedding, to get set up in that city. We were talking about going out there together to do some serious house-hunting and to find a place to live. The money they were offering made it possible for us to think like that. It was a great setup for us, on every level. It was, in many ways, the job of a lifetime for me," Jamie admits.

As you've probably guessed, the potential move was vetoed by Jamie's mother, who did not directly prevent her son from moving away, but instead guilted him into staying nearby where he could be helpful and available to her. She was persuasive and manipulative without giving her son a direct order.

"I'll never see you again," Jamie remembers his mother telling him at the time. "And I don't know what I'll do with this great big old house, with things breaking down all the time, with so much needing repair and attention.

"I guess I could get remarried or something," his mother continued. "But I've never loved any man the way I loved your father. I don't think I could ever love anyone that way again.

"If you move away, I won't have anyone left!" Jamie's mother lamented.

Jamie remembers trying to explain to his mother that, with the high salary his new job would provide, he could visit her often, and he could care for her well.

"I don't want your money, I want you right here by my side," is how Jamie remembers his mother's response.

Megan jumps in with her affirmation.

"That's exactly what she said. I remember her using that exact phrase, that she wanted Jamie by her side. And even then, while we weren't even married yet, I remember thinking that was kind of a weird thing to say. I mean, Jamie was about to join *me* at *my side!* Don't you think a groom should be at the side of his bride, not at the side of his mother?"

Jamie stares at the floor.

"I don't think Mom realizes she's manipulating me all the time," Jamie says finally, after a very long pause. "I don't think she's trying to ruin our romantic relationship either. I think she's just lonely, and she keeps making up all these excuses to have me come over there so she won't be lonely."

Megan concurs. "I'm sure that's true," she says softly. "But the solution to your mother's loneliness shouldn't come at the expense of our marriage.

"If your mom doesn't want to remarry, that's fine. It's her life, and it's her choice. But if she's lonely, she can definitely get out and meet people, make new friends, be more involved at church, and lots of things like that. There are so many ways she can interact with people, so many ways she can be a part of life instead of being off to the side of life like she is now."

Megan is warming to her topic. Her voice is getting louder, and she is putting more energy into her sudden narrative.

"I'm fine with both of us—as a couple—going over to your mom's house every Saturday for the rest of our lives. I would do that every Saturday forever! We could go over there as a couple and we could do all the chores she could find for us to do. Except for a rare emergency—and let's face it, none of your mom's calls have been true emergencies—your mother could just save up all her little household chores until we came over there every Saturday."

Jamie is listening attentively.

"That way," Megan continues, "we'd be doing this together as a couple, we'd be making life better for your mom, and everything would be great! And even more important, you and I would have our evenings together, in our own house, as a husband and wife." Megan looks directly at her husband, clearly drawing his gaze.

"What I need to hear from you," she tells him, "is that our relationship as husband and wife is more important to you than your relationship with your mom."

Jamie makes one of the wisest decisions of his life. Without hesitation he replies affirmatively to his wife's challenge.

"Honey," Jamie says, reaching out to hug and hold his wife. "There's no question about that. Not at all. You are far more important to me than my mother could ever be. I'm sorry I've been spending so much time away from you, and I'm ready to do whatever it takes to be home more often. I need to be less distracted by my mom's constant phone calls and constant little nonemergencies!"

Megan, sensing her husband's truthfulness and intentions, lets out a long sigh of relief, embracing her life partner with genuine affection.

"That's what I'm talking about," Megan says, visibly relaxing. "I'm talking about you and me, instead of you and her."

* * *

When we marry a life partner, we marry his or her parents, siblings, and extended relatives. We marry his or her family history, family patterns, and family values. Before we know it, we find ourselves creating a new family that is very much impacted by the family history that has gone before us.

Familiar patterns emerge and repeat themselves.

Familiar problems surface and disrupt our relationships.

Understanding our families is critically important as we plan a marriage, establish a new home, and confront the reality of forming a new family together.

The clues to our own family's future can be found in the family histories that each of us brings into the new union.

With that in mind, following are topics of discussion that can help you explore what family has meant to each of you in terms of relationships, duties, and ongoing connections.

As we do so, let's look at key areas in which family differences are likely to cause stress or difficulty in a new relationship. Some of the most important areas of difference are among the topics of discussion included.

Family XPR Discussion Questions

1. Each of you answer the following questions: Which family member, among all of your relatives, is the most likely to pressure you to have children? Why is this so? How will you respond to this family member when the subject comes up? Which family member, among all of your relatives, seems the least likely to pressure you about anything at all, and the most likely to simply accept you as you are? What kind of person are you? Do you pressure others to conform to your ideas and values, or do you tend to accept and value people just as they are?

2. Each of you answer the following questions: Based on your experience with your family of origin, which family member, among all of your relatives, is the most likely to want or hope that you will stay nearby and live in the same general area as they do? Why is this so? Do you believe that this kind of pressure helps a family stay together, or do you see this kind of family pressure as a negative force? Explain your answer. How does your family react when a family member moves away? Has this actually happened?

3. How does your family show affection for one another? Does your family say "I love you" to each other, or is that expression rare and usually a very private matter? Does your family hug each other when arriving or departing? Did your parents display physical affection for each other in front of the children while you were growing up? Would you describe your father as loving and affectionate? Why or why not? Would you describe your mother as loving and affectionate? Why or why not?

4. How often does your family give out friendly and positive compliments to one another? Did you grow up receiving verbal praise and spoken affirmations when you achieved something, succeeded at something, or brought home a good grade? Did you grow up hearing a father or mother praise you and compliment you for your appearance, your character, your success, or some other aspect of your personality? Or was your family slow to give praise, perhaps believing that praising a child would only lead to unhealthy pride? How does your family express compliments to one another? Do you believe your family of origin is pretty much in balance in the ways in which they express compliments?

5. Which holidays does your family gather together to celebrate? Do they gather for each birthday as it occurs? Do they gather for special holidays, such as Christmas, Easter, Thanksgiving? Do they also tend to gather any time there's a holiday, including the Fourth of July, Presidents' Day, and other lesser holidays? Does your family believe that after you are married you and your spouse will continue to be present for birthdays, holidays, and special events?

6. Does your family take vacations together or have an annual family reunion somewhere? Have any of your siblings married before you? If so, have they continued the pattern of getting together for a family vacation or a family reunion? Does your family believe that after your marriage you and your spouse will be present at family reunions and will join other members of the family for family vacations?

7. Will your parents or family members be visiting you as overnight guests in your home after you are married? Do they expect that you will host them appreciatively and often? Do they simply assume that they are welcome to visit whenever they wish and to stay as long as they like? How do your own personal opinions on this topic compare with the opinions of your family? How would you explain to a family member that it should not be assumed that your home is always available for visits?

8. Does your family automatically expect that after you are married you and your spouse will attend the same local church they attend? If the local church is different, does your family at least assume that you will attend a church of the same denomination? How would your family react if you married someone whose religious affiliation was substantially different from theirs? How does your family feel about regular church attendance as a sign and proof that someone is truly religious?

9. At election time, does your family of origin tend to all side with one political party or with one kind of ideology? For example, is everyone in your family a Republican? A Democrat? Is everyone in your family of origin basically a conservative? A liberal? Have you seen any family member try to break away from the established pattern? If so, how was he or she received after making a change in the family's voting pattern, party affiliation, or ideological perspective? How would your family react if your new partner had vastly different political opinions than the ones he or she holds? Is your family open and accepting of other values, including political beliefs, or

do they judge others on the basis of whether or not they agree with the family's views?

10. Within your family of origin, have you ever heard ideas or values expressed that seemed racist or judgmental about race? Has anyone in your immediate family ever married someone from another culture or of another race? If so, how did the family respond to this? If you wished to marry someone of another race, how would your family react and respond? Why? If you wished to adopt children of another race, how would your family respond? Does your family tend to believe that some races are better than others? Do you agree with your family's perspective on this? Why or why not?

10
FAMILY

*Your Premarriage **Expectations** About Family Life*

"His mother is over here every single day!" Rachel exclaims, letting out a loud sigh. "I mean, I like her, but enough is enough!

"She keeps finding reasons to drop in. She'll bring us some cookies or stop by with some mail that came for Blake at the house. It's not like it's a crisis or an emergency or something. It's like any excuse will do, she just wants to be over here in our apartment all the time!"

Beside her, Blake isn't saying very much. He considers his words carefully before he begins framing a response. He looks at the counselor, hoping to find some sympathy and some understanding for his own perspective.

"Since the divorce, Mom has been kind of lonely," Blake begins. He gets no farther before his wife quickly interrupts him.

"I know she's lonely, and I really do love her," Rachel responds. "I honestly like your mother, and I want to be her friend. But not every day! Not twice a day sometimes! And definitely not in my own home! I'm sick of it!"

Rachel looks at the counselor, wondering if she should continue.

The counselor, in turn, looks directly at Blake.

"Blake, before we talk about this in detail, why do you think your mom stops by so often? Why do you think she keeps coming over to your apartment?"

"Well, I kind of told her she was welcome in our home any time," Blake says quietly, looking at the floor. "I mean, I felt sorry for her being all alone. I'm the baby of the family and the last one to leave the house. Without me there, she has no one, and I'm sure she gets lonely and misses my dad.

"So I told her we loved her and she was welcome any time. But, really, I didn't mean every day! I love my mom to death, but seeing her every day drives me crazy too. I just don't know what to do about it! I'm the one who told her she was welcome at our place any time. I'm the one who really caused this problem, but I have no idea how to get out of it. I don't think we can!"

Blake leans forward in his chair, staring at the floor, waiting for a rebuke from his wife, the counselor, or both.

* * *

Thousands of miles away in Central America, Aricela and Pedro would love to have Rachel and Blake's problem. They would love to have their own apartment, their own personal space, a home to call their own. They wouldn't mind if Pedro's mother stopped by their home every day. A life like that would be a big improvement over their current situation.

Pedro, the oldest of seven children, was the first one of his siblings to get married. Just as Pedro was about to walk down the aisle and get married to Aricela, Pedro's father was hurt in a tragic accident at the tire factory where he worked. Although Pedro's father survived the accident, he was no longer able to keep working due to the terrible injuries he received. Pedro's father is physically handicapped, and depending on how his healing and recovery proceed, he may never be able to do factory work again.

Because of the father's injury, Pedro and Aricela canceled their plans to have a place of their own. After the wedding they moved into Pedro's family home. Pedro's mother immediately went out and found a job; she's now gone all day and works cleaning houses in an upscale neighborhood nearby. Her income is much less than Pedro's father earned, yet the family is surviving financially.

Since Pedro's mother is out of the house all day, Aricela is the one who does the difficult work of caring for Pedro's father and the entire family. Aricela, newly married to a man she truly loves, finds herself cooking, cleaning, and parenting Pedro's six younger siblings, as well as caring for her physically injured father-in-law who has many needs. Even for a strong young woman who loves her husband and his family, this type of life is exhausting. The work never ends; each new sunrise brings Aricela a fresh realization of how much difficulty she will face in the long day ahead.

"I don't want to seem ungrateful," Aricela says to a counselor. "I know a lot of people have more troubles than me. But I always thought my husband and I would have a little home of our own when we got married. I always thought we would have children of our own, and I would be raising my own children someday.

"Instead, I am raising six children who are not even mine! And I am caring for an old man who is injured and in pain and can't help himself. I am doing all of the cooking and all of the cleaning and all of the work there is to do around the house. When Celia, my mother-in-law, comes home, she's tired from cleaning other people's houses all day. So she just sits down and plays with her children and doesn't do anything to help me. She just watches me work.

"I don't blame her. I know how tired she is, but this is not the life I expected! This is not the life I wanted. How can I say this? I am trying not to feel sorry for myself all the time, but some days I just want to walk right out the door and never come back! Some days, even though I love these people, I just want to say 'I quit!' and walk out the door. Then maybe they would realize how much I do for them all the time."

✳ ✳ ✳

Can you identify at all with these two wives, thousands of miles apart, as they experience married life in a way they never imagined? Now that you've met Aricela, you may have forgotten about Rachel's problem, which may seem a bit minor to you by comparison—almost trivial. But to Rachel, the constant and unwelcome intrusions from her mother-in-law are extremely frustrating. Rachel has lost her joy.

We included Aricela and Pedro's story in this book for a variety of reasons, with the hope that their condition as newlyweds might help you feel better about your own challenges or your own future. Can you imagine being newly married, living in the same home as your husband's family, and functionally becoming the mother, cook, janitor, home health nurse all at once? Can you think for a moment how Aricela must feel?

Whether you are a man or a woman, think for a moment about Pedro's life. He is a normal, healthy young male. He was looking forward to having his own wife and his own life so that he could enjoy the benefits of being married. Now he lives in the same house that he grew up in.

When Pedro comes home from his job selling cell phones, this is what he walks into. His wife, who is beautiful and who loves him very much, is exhausted from her never-ending work. She has lost her energy, and she is rarely happy or smiling. So Pedro, who expected married life to be fun and lighthearted and full of sexual intimacy, is finding that his real life is much different than he expected. He knows that his wife loves him, but he rarely gets to experience her love in a sexual way. During their rare moments of intimacy, he is very conscious of the need to be quiet so that the rest of the family is not aware of the couple's lovemaking.

Pedro feels sorry for his wife because of her exhausting work. But when he is honest, as he was with the counselor, Pedro also feels sorry for himself!

Does Pedro's perspective seem selfish or short-sighted to you, or can you understand how a young husband might be a little frustrated while living in this type of situation? Yes, he suffers far less than Aricela does. But as a young husband, he is missing out on most of what he thought marriage would bring to him. If you are a male, it may be easier to identify with Pedro's suffering in this case.

Pedro has almost no privacy and very little time with his attractive young wife. Pedro, who hoped to escape his siblings and his family and his home, instead finds himself living in the very same bedroom as before. It's as if he never grew up after all. He is still a brother and a son, instead of the husband and father and head of the household he intended to be.

Pedro believes he is missing out on the respect he deserves, and the deeper issue is that he does not respect himself. Instead, he blames himself for the troubles that his wife is facing and the conditions in the family home day after day.

* * *

Meanwhile, Rachel is telling her husband what needs to change. She is giving him clear instructions as to the next steps in solving their problem.

"Blake, I need you to tell your mother that we love her, but we are newlyweds who need a little more space," Rachel begins. "If I tell her something like that, she'll just think that her new daughter-in-law doesn't love her, but if you tell her that as her son, maybe she will listen to you and stop coming over here all the time."

Blake does not make eye contact with his wife. "I don't see how I could possibly tell my mom something like that," he begins, squirming in his chair and focusing on the floor. "I mean, how would I bring that up? And how is Mom going to feel if I tell her she's not welcome over here? She's all alone in the world, and being around us cheers her up a little bit. How can I take away the one thing in her life that seems to make her happy? How is that fair to her, or a help to her?

"Maybe you should talk to her," Blake counters, still not looking at his wife. "Maybe you should be the one to tell her, and then I'll come along and reassure her that we still love her and everything."

Blake looks at the counselor, hoping to find an ally and a friend. Today at least, Blake will be disappointed in that quest.

* * *

Pedro is apologizing to his wife. "If I had known how things would work out, I would have never asked you to marry me," Pedro begins, stammering. He is looking at his wife as he speaks. "I mean, I love you very much, and I will always love you, but there is no way I wanted you to have to work so hard or to live with my family! This is not how I wanted our life to go. Some days I wish I had never proposed to you, and then you wouldn't be caught up in all of this drama!

"You could still be living your life, free and easy. I would be working, but maybe one of my sisters could step up and help with the children or do some of the cooking or the cleaning." Pedro looks at his wife; he seems to be near tears as he is talking to her.

"I am so sorry I got you into all of this. In a way, this is all my fault! If I had never asked you to marry me, you would not be living in so much difficulty. You would not be working so hard. You would not be suffering so greatly." Pedro slumps in his chair.

Beside him, Aricela reaches over to take his hand.

"This is not your fault," she tells her husband. "This is not your fault. But I cannot go on living this way. I am sorry to be so selfish, but I cannot keep living like this, and I do not know what to do. I am tired all the time, I end up yelling at your little brothers, and by the end of the day I do not even like myself. I do not like the person I am turning into, day after day after day.

"When I look in the mirror, I do not see a person I respect. I see someone who is tired and worn out and just wants to escape all this.

"I love you," Aricela says quietly to her husband. "I will always love you. But sometimes I just want to run away from everything—including you—and never come back. I know how evil that must sound to you, but that is how I feel."

Pedro hugs his wife and holds her close to him. "You are not evil," he whispers. "You are my wife, and I love you."

* * *

Life can surprise us.

It is impossible to predict the future; anything might happen. No one knows when a relative or family member might be injured or become ill; it may be difficult or impossible to foresee a divorce coming in the immediate family. So many things are out of our control, it's important for each of us to take personal responsibility for the things that we can control.

How can a couple wisely prepare for marriage, if life is unpredictable?

One way is by clearly expressing our expectations, allowing our partner to hear our hearts and understand our perspectives. And whether we are talking about money or intimacy or settling our conflicts, we'll be involved with family life for a very long time, which means that life in the family is something we simply must talk about as we prepare to join our lives with someone else.

As has been stated, when you marry someone you are not just marrying a solitary spouse, you are also marrying that person's network of family and relatives, that person's context of relationships and obligations. It is highly important to understand how your potential partner relates to his or her family and to his or her duties within the family system.

Family systems and family styles will matter over the long haul, and these systems and styles are fairly resistant to change.

Your new husband's family will probably keep on being just as it is after you marry him. Your wife's relatives will probably continue their personal styles and personal preferences after your wedding. So it's important for you to not only meet the family but also get to know the family and how family members relate to each other and others outside the family.

Sit down as a couple and explore your future within the family systems you bring to the marriage. As divorce and remarriage keep expanding the family circle, take a look at the various networks you'll be joining and the types of expectations you may be facing from parents, stepparents, and the grandparents of your future children. Life in a family is complex and challenging; thinking through these issues in advance can help you be prepared.

Your Family XPT Discussion

1. Think about Rachel and Blake's situation from Rachel's perspective. She's a young wife, and she may be insecure about how she cooks, cleans, or decorates her apartment. Every day, without advance notice, Rachel's mother-in-law stops by, usually with some excuse about cookies or mail or something else. How would you feel if you were Rachel? How do you believe Rachel should work to resolve this issue? What needs to change here?

2. Now think about Rachel and Blake's situation from Blake's perspective. He loves his mother, and he cares about her well-being. His mother is recently divorced and no longer has children at home. Blake was the last child to leave the nest, which means his mother is now alone in her home. In an act of love and compassion,

Blake told his mother she was welcome in his new home anytime. Clearly, Blake didn't mean every day, but now he's already extended the invitation. Can he rescind it or take back his words somehow? Will he offend his mother if he does? Think about this situation from Blake's perspective rather than Rachel's, and explore what he might do to resolve this issue. Do you see Blake as having the primary responsibility to make things better? Can he do so while still loving and affirming his mother?

3. As you prepare to be married, do you expect to be living near your wife's parents or family members? If so, about how often do you expect to see them? Do you expect to host them in your home or do you imagine that you'll mostly be visiting them in their own house or apartment? If your wife's family was visiting you in your new home once a week, would that seem too seldom, too frequent, or just about right? If you were dining at your wife's parents' home once a week after getting married, does that seem about the right frequency for seeing them and being with them?

4. Now answer the previous question by thinking about the husband's parents and relatives. As you prepare to be married, do you expect to be living near your husband's parents or family members? If so, about how often do you expect to see them? Do you expect to host them in your home or do you imagine that you'll mostly be visiting them in their own house or apartment? If your husband's family was visiting you in your home once a week, would that seem too seldom, too frequent, or just about right? If you were dining at your husband's par-

ents' home once a week after getting married, does that seem about the right frequency for seeing them and being with them?

5. After your marriage, will you be living in the same home as either of your parents or family members? This kind of housing arrangement is typical for newlyweds in many countries and in many cultures. Increasingly, we see this trend in North America and Western Europe due to the high cost of housing and a global economy that is facing challenges. If this will be your situation, about how long do you expect you will be living with family members? What is your plan for getting a place of your own? Do you have one? What kinds of actions must be taken in order for you to have your own apartment or house?

6. If you will be living with other relatives or family members after your wedding, how will this impact your privacy and time together as a couple? How will you achieve privacy while living under the same roof as other relatives and family members? What kinds of boundaries or patterns should you establish, right from the start, if you want to have privacy and intimacy as a couple? How will you avoid being frustrated by intrusions into your space or family expectations regarding your time while living in the same home? What conversations might you need to have, in advance, to establish some boundaries?

7. Think about Aricela and Pedro's situation from the perspective of the tired, overworked young wife. Should she resign herself to ten or twenty years of hard labor? Should she expect to raise Pedro's brothers and sisters as if they were her own children? Should she postpone

having children of her own, since she is so busy caring for her nieces and nephews? Should she quit feeling sorry for herself and just get to work, thinking only of others? Or can you understand how frustrated she feels, how ready she is to just run away? How would you advise her, if you were Aricela's best friend?

8. Think about Aricela and Pedro's situation from the perspective of the caring but seemingly trapped young husband. At times he feels sorry for himself because he is a young married man living without the benefits of being married. He has physical and sexual needs that are unmet. At the same time, he feels terribly sorry that he has inflicted this difficult situation on his young wife, whom he truly loves. Can you feel what Pedro feels and understand his perspective in this challenging situation? If you were Pedro's friend, how might you advise him to proceed? Should he and his wife move out of the parents' home and begin a life of their own? What can Pedro do to make things better for his wife and for himself, or is he simply trapped in this disaster for the next few years or longer? Is there any way out?

9. If something happened to your new partner's parents, and the result was that one of the parents was widowed or divorced or was older and needed daily care, would you invite that parent to come and live with you? Would your invitation be short-term or open-ended? How would you feel if one of your partner's parents moved into your home and lived with you for years? How would you feel if one of your own parents moved in with you and lived with you for years? How likely is this to hap-

pen? How prepared are you for these kinds of setbacks and situations? Have either of you already expressed to a parent or a family member that he or she is welcome to move in with you if something like that should happen? Talk together about this possibility.

10. Is it a burden or a blessing to be connected with relatives and family members? Are there more benefits than duties when you are part of a larger family? Do the obligations and the requirements weigh you down, causing you to forget about the blessings and the bonuses?

11. Think about old age, being widowed or divorced or in poor health, from the perspective of the older person. Would you personally wish to move in with your children or grandchildren if you were older, in poor health, or suddenly divorced? Would you expect your children to welcome you warmly and openly into their home? Would you be angry if your children did not quickly and warmly make a place for you to come and live with them? How might you feel if your children expected you to simply solve your own problems as you age, become unhealthy, or are divorced or widowed?

12. It comes down to this: what do we owe each other as family members? When do our obligations as children end? How can we carry out our true responsibilities in a way that preserves and protects our own marriage, our own children, and our own identities? As you think and talk about these things, are both of you on the same page with regard to family duties, family responsibilities, and family expectations? Can you bring a united perspective into any future discussions with relatives and

family members as they try to make demands on your time, your money, or your housing arrangements? How will you respond to these kinds of demands, requests, or problems?

RIGHT FROM THE START
Recommended Reading

Sexuality and Intimacy

Sheet Music
Kevin Lehman
Tyndale House Publishers, 2003

The Soul-Mate Marriage: The Spiritual Journey of Becoming One
David and Lisa Frisbie
Harvest House Publishers, 2009

Intended for Pleasure
Ed Wheat
Revell House, 3rd Edition, 1997

The Act of Marriage
Tim LaHaye
Zondervan Publishers, Revised Edition 1998

The Gift of Sex: A Guide to Sexual Fulfillment
Clifford and Joyce Penner
Thomas Nelson Publishers, Revised Edition, 2003

What Wives Wish Their Husbands Knew About Sex
Ryan Howes, Richard Rupp, Steven Simpson
Baker Books, 2007

Is That All He Thinks About?: How to Enjoy Great Sex with Your Husband
Marla Taviano
Harvest House Publishers, 2007

No More Headaches: Enjoying Sex and Intimacy in Marriage
Juli Slattery
Tyndale House Publishers, 2009

Money and Finances

The Total Money Makeover: A Proven Plan for Financial Fitness
Dave Ramsey
Thomas Nelson Publishers, 2009

Faith-Based Family Finances: Let Go of Worry and Grow in Confidence
Ron Blue, Jeremy White
Tyndale House Publishers, 2008

The Complete Financial Guide for Young Couples: A Lifetime Approach to Spending, Saving, and Investing
Larry Burkett
David C. Cook Publishers, 2002

Money and Marriage God's Way
Howard Dayton
Moody Press Publishers, 2009

Money, Possessions, and Eternity
Randy Alcorn
Tyndale House Publishers, 2003

Family Financial Workbook
Larry Burkett
Moody Press Publishers, 2002

The Burkett and Blue Definitive Guide to Securing Wealth to Last: Money Essentials for the Second Half of Life
Larry Burkett, Ron Blue, Jeremy White
B & H Publishing Group, 2003

Power and Control Issues

Trading Places: The Best Move You'll Ever Make in Your Marriage
Les Parrott and Leslie Parrott
Zondervan Publishers, 2008

Happily Remarried: Making Decisions Together, Blending a Family, Building a Love That Will Last
David and Lisa Frisbie
Harvest House Publishers, 2005

Love and Respect: The Love She Most Desires, the Respect He Desperately Needs
Emerson Eggerichs
Thomas Nelson Publishers, 2004

His Needs, Her Needs: Building an Affair-Proof Marriage
Willard Harley
Revell Publishers, 15th Edition, 2001

The DNA of Relationships
Gary Smalley
Tyndale House Publishers, 2007

A Lasting Promise: A Christian Guide to Fighting for Your Marriage
Scott Stanley, Daniel Trathen, Savanna McCain, Milt Bryan
Jossey Bass Publishers, 1998

Faith, Values, and Spirituality

Sacred Marriage
Gary Thomas
Zondervan Publishers, 2000

The Soul-Mate Marriage: The Spiritual Journey of Becoming One
David and Lisa Frisbie
Harvest House Publishers, 2009

This Momentary Marriage: A Parable of Permanence
John Piper
Crossway Books Publisher, 2009

What Did You Expect? Redeeming the Realities of Marriage
Paul Tripp
Crossway Books Publisher, 2010

God, Marriage, and Family: Rebuilding the Biblical Foundation
Andreas Kostenberger, David Jones
Crossway Books Publisher, 2010

Making a Marriage: Seven Essentials for a Strong Relationship
David and Lisa Frisbie, Jim Pettitt, Roger Hahn, edited by Larry
Morris
Beacon Hill Press of Kansas City, 2006

Family Life and Relationships

Relationships: How to Make Bad Relationships Better and Good Relationships Great
Les Parrott and Leslie Parrott
Zondervan Publishers, 2002

The Soul-Mate Marriage: The Spiritual Journey of Becoming One
David and Lisa Frisbie
Harvest House Publishers, 2009

Covenant Marriage: Building Communication and Intimacy
Gary Chapman
B & H Publishing Group, 2003

The Ten Commandments of Marriage
Beth Moore, Ed Young
Moody Press Publishers, 2004

Lord, Change My Attitude: Before It's Too Late
James MacDonald, Erwin Lutzer
Moody Press Publishers, 2008

In-Law Relationships: The Chapman Guide to Becoming Friends with Your In-Laws
Gary Chapman
Tyndale House Publishers, 2008

Becoming Your Husband's Best Friend
David and Lisa Frisbie
Harvest House Publishers, 2011

ABOUT THE AUTHORS

David and Lisa Frisbie jointly serve as executive directors of the Center for Marriage and Family Studies in Del Mar, California. Widely recognized and frequently quoted experts on marriage and family life, they have traveled to all fifty of the United States, nine provinces and two territories of Canada, and more than forty world nations to teach, speak, and train leaders. They have an active interest in serving pastors, missionaries, and other leaders, and have been featured presenters at retreats for pastors and missionaries in North America and Western, Central, and Southeastern Europe. They have also worked with candidate screening, orientation, debriefing, and other counseling of field workers and leaders for various organizations.

The authors are alumni of MidAmerica Nazarene University and have authored or coauthored fourteen books and dozens of articles in journals and mainstream magazines.

Married since 1978, David and Lisa travel to speak, teach, and counsel. Their life focus is helping marriages and families become healthy, and they have a special interest in serving the families of pastors, missionaries, and others in full-time Christian service.

To request the authors to speak at your event, contact Lisa Douglas at mountainmediagroup@yahoo.com.

The Frisbies' literary agent is Rachelle Gardner, Rachelle@WordServeAgency.com.

For publicity, media events, and book signings by the authors, contact Laurie Tomlinson at Laurie@keymgc.com.

"Let's make a special effort to stop communicating with each other, so we can have some conversation." —Mark Twain

In *Couple Conversation,* marriage and family therapist Theodore Chaffee shows couples how to create a sensuous, smart, and deeply intimate relationship by building on the four dimensions of the human experience: body, mind, soul, and spirit. With informal explanations, an array of illustrations, and splashes of humor, Chaffee explores each dimension's purpose and helps couples discover new ways to use conversation to confidently develop intimacy in every aspect of their relationship.

Couple Conversation
The Art of Creating Intimacy
Theodore Chaffee
ISBN: 978-0-8341-2374-8

BEACON HILL PRESS
OF KANSAS CITY

Find time to grow.

Making a Marriage addresses the issues faced by new as well as mature couples from a biblical point of view and offers the foundational principles that help build a strong and lasting relationship. Written by educators and licensed counselors, this valuable resource educates couples on the essentials of marriage so they can honor their lifelong vows, improve their relationships with their spouses, and counter our culture's destructive influences.

Making a Marriage
7 Essentials for a Strong Relationship
Edited by Larry R. Morris
Stories by David and Lisa Frisbie, Jim Pettitt, Roger Hahn, et al.
ISBN: 978-0-8341-2301-4

BEACON HILL PRESS
OF KANSAS CITY

www.beaconhillbooks.com
Available online or wherever books are sold.